Organizations: A Very Short Introduction

VERY SHORT INTRODUCTIONS are for anyone wanting a stimulating and accessible way in to a new subject. They are written by experts, and have been published in more than 25 languages worldwide.

The series began in 1995, and now represents a wide variety of topics in history, philosophy, religion, science, and the humanities. The VSI Library now contains over 200 volumes—a Very Short Introduction to everything from ancient Egypt and Indian philosophy to conceptual art and cosmology—and will continue to grow to a library of around 300 titles.

Very Short Introductions available now:

ADVERTISING  Winston Fletcher
AFRICAN HISTORY
    John Parker and Richard Rathbone
AGNOSTICISM  Robin Le Poidevin
AMERICAN POLITICAL PARTIES
    AND ELECTIONS  L. Sandy Maisel
THE AMERICAN PRESIDENCY
    Charles O. Jones
ANARCHISM  Colin Ward
ANCIENT EGYPT  Ian Shaw
ANCIENT PHILOSOPHY  Julia Annas
ANCIENT WARFARE
    Harry Sidebottom
ANGLICANISM  Mark Chapman
THE ANGLO-SAXON AGE  John Blair
ANIMAL RIGHTS  David DeGrazia
ANTISEMITISM  Steven Beller
THE APOCRYPHAL GOSPELS
    Paul Foster
ARCHAEOLOGY  Paul Bahn
ARCHITECTURE  Andrew Ballantyne
ARISTOCRACY  William Doyle
ARISTOTLE  Jonathan Barnes
ART HISTORY  Dana Arnold
ART THEORY  Cynthia Freeland
ATHEISM  Julian Baggini
AUGUSTINE  Henry Chadwick
AUTISM  Uta Frith
BARTHES  Jonathan Culler
BEAUTY  Roger Scruton
BESTSELLERS  John Sutherland
THE BIBLE  John Riches
BIBLICAL ARCHEOLOGY  Eric H. Cline
BIOGRAPHY  Hermione Lee

THE BLUES  Elijah Wald
THE BOOK OF MORMON
    Terryl Givens
THE BRAIN  Michael O'Shea
BRITISH POLITICS  Anthony Wright
BUDDHA  Michael Carrithers
BUDDHISM  Damien Keown
BUDDHIST ETHICS  Damien Keown
CAPITALISM  James Fulcher
CATHOLICISM  Gerald O'Collins
THE CELTS  Barry Cunliffe
CHAOS  Leonard Smith
CHOICE THEORY  Michael Allingham
CHRISTIAN ART  Beth Williamson
CHRISTIAN ETHICS  D. Stephen Long
CHRISTIANITY  Linda Woodhead
CITIZENSHIP  Richard Bellamy
CLASSICAL MYTHOLOGY
    Helen Morales
CLASSICS
    Mary Beard and John Henderson
CLAUSEWITZ  Michael Howard
THE COLD WAR  Robert McMahon
COMMUNISM  Leslie Holmes
CONSCIOUSNESS
    Susan Blackmore
CONTEMPORARY ART
    Julian Stallabrass
CONTINENTAL PHILOSOPHY
    Simon Critchley
COSMOLOGY  Peter Coles
CRITICAL THEORY  Stephen Bronner
THE CRUSADES
    Christopher Tyerman

Available soon:

For more information visit our web site
www.oup.com/vsi/

Mary Jo Hatch

# ORGANIZATIONS

## A Very Short Introduction

OXFORD
UNIVERSITY PRESS

# OXFORD

## UNIVERSITY PRESS

Great Clarendon Street, Oxford OX2 6DP

Oxford University Press is a department of the University of Oxford.
It furthers the University's objective of excellence in research, scholarship,
and education by publishing worldwide in

Oxford New York

Auckland Cape Town Dar es Salaam Hong Kong Karachi
Kuala Lumpur Madrid Melbourne Mexico City Nairobi
New Delhi Shanghai Taipei Toronto

With offices in

Argentina Austria Brazil Chile Czech Republic France Greece
Guatemala Hungary Italy Japan Poland Portugal Singapore
South Korea Switzerland Thailand Turkey Ukraine Vietnam

Oxford is a registered trade mark of Oxford University Press
in the UK and in certain other countries

Published in the United States
by Oxford University Press Inc., New York

© Mary Jo Hatch 2011

British Library Cataloguing in Publication Data

Data available

Library of Congress Cataloging in Publication Data

Data available

Typeset by SPI Publisher Services, Pondicherry, India
Printed in Great Britain by
Ashford Colour Press Ltd, Gosport, Hampshire

ISBN 978-0-19-958453-6

1 3 5 7 9 10 8 6 4 2

# Contents

*To all the organizers*

# Preface

Organizing is interesting because everyone does it. You may not be conscious of having organized anything, but I bet you have. Ever arranged your desk or closet so you could more easily find your stuff? How about creating a filing system? Perhaps you organized a play or festival, threw a party, or led your friends in a collective game of dodge ball or fantasy football. Are you part of a family? A church? Ever attended school? If so, you have been a member of one or more organizations. Maybe you have a job working in a small business or for a big corporation, a government agency, or a charity. Then you've seen organization from the inside.

Organizations are everywhere, and organizing is a key activity in life. With or without consciousness of this fact, it remains true. Knowing something about organizing can be useful and fascinating. This book will serve as an entry point and guide to thinking about organizations and organizing. It will build on your experiences and reveal things about the many organizations you have met that you probably never thought about before. In it you will find insights into your experiences as well as stories based on mine to enliven your reading.

This book is intended for a general audience. You will need little or no prior knowledge of the subject matter, but if you already have some, I am sure you will find the book a handy review that provokes new insight. Throughout you will encounter some fairly abstract ideas, but I will ground these with concrete examples and in this way guide you through the more complicated ideas about organizations in a gentle way. Curiosity is all that is required for you to have a rich and rewarding reading experience.

You will also meet some of the greatest organizational thinkers and the ideas that they contributed to the study of organizations. There are too many to tell you about all of them, so I chose the ones I thought you would most like to tell your friends or colleagues about. Anytime you meet someone new you will learn when they lived so that you can see how far back into history the knowledge of organizations reaches and also get a sense of the order in which ideas were introduced.

My suggestion is that you read this book straight through (it's short!), with the aim to get the big picture. Then look back through the chapters again. It is more fun to think about organizations when you have a few concepts to mix together, and the ideas will connect as they spend a little time in your brain, where they can work on each other like a good stew. Simmering ideas brings out flavorful nuances and will refine your taste in ideas.

The ideas about organizations and organizing have long amazed me with the insight they bring when applied, not just to work, but to life in general. I hope the ideas presented in this *Very Short Introduction* will amaze and delight you, and that you will find many uses for what you learn about organizations to help you now and in the future.

Mary Jo Hatch
Ipswich, Massachusetts
14 November 2010

# Acknowledgements

First, I would like to thank my husband, organizational psychologist Philip Mirvis, for taking the time to carefully read and thoroughly critique the final manuscript of this book. My dear friend and neighbor Helen Danforth, a musician, was also more than generous with her time in reading a complete draft and providing many helpful comments and ideas, including several thoughtful insights about music. Professor Ulla Johansson, my colleague at Gothenburg University's Business and Design Lab, and Kaj Sköldberg from the Stockholm School of Business provided encouragement and suggestions for writing about power in organizations. Thanks also go to my editors at Oxford University Press, Andrea Keegan, David Musson, Emma Marchant, and Helen Hill, as well as to the anonymous reviewers who approved this project and helped guide it to completion. Finally, I express deep gratitude to Sri Harold Klemp, the Mahanta, the Living ECK Master, who taught me that truth should be delivered in as many dimensions as possible. May you find some of them here.

# List of illustrations

Organizations

# Chapter 1
# **What is organization?**

Organization happens when people work together to accomplish some desired end state or goal. It can happen through intentionally designed activity, spontaneous improvisation, or some combination of the two, but it always depends upon coordinated effort. As a simple example, think about the goal of moving a large stone, too big for one human working alone to push uphill (Figure 1a). Two or even more won't budge it either (Figure 1b), unless they coordinate their efforts (Figure 1c).

But people often pursue more complex goals than pushing a stone uphill. Putting Neil Armstrong and Buzz Aldrin on the Moon meant coordinating everything from cleaning offices and buying paperclips to training the astronauts and designing, building, and launching their spacecraft. Supplying the Tsukiji Fish Market in Tokyo (Japan) that serves the restaurants and fishmongers of the world depends on the coordinated efforts of fishing crews that sail off the coasts of Cartagena (Spain), Halifax (Canada), Boston (US), and Pusan (South Korea), and on the mostly Japanese buyers who fly to these places to survey the catch, purchase the best fish available, and crate and ship them to Tokyo. As these examples show, the coordination of human interests and activities can range from the simple to the massively complex, and its goals from the mundane to the exotic.

1. **Getting organized:** The person in a) confronts a problem too big to handle alone, moving a large stone to the top of a hill; b) finds help but does not use it in a coordinated way and so the stone remains at the bottom of the hill; c) organizes the actions of those who came to help and achieves the desired outcome

## A little history

Organizing has been with us a long time. Prehistoric humans organized to hunt and gather food, find shelter, and protect and raise their children. To nurture their souls they made art and practiced religion. By grouping together in pursuing these goals, they formed the first human organizations – families and tribes. Of course, chimpanzees and apes banded together before humans appeared, and prior to that ants formed colonies and bees built hives. On some level, all social species realize that organizing improves their chances for survival in a competitive ecology. Through organization the strength and creativity of many can be directed toward survival or civilization via developments in technology and the accumulation of economic and cultural wealth.

Competition is as important to organization as is cooperation. This might seem contradictory, but it is not. Competition arises from dependence on the environment to provide food and to feed other needs and desires. If resources were unlimited, then the drive to organize might be minimal. If food dropped off trees, the climate was temperate all year round, and nothing tried to kill us, we might get by with only those forms of organization required to amuse or enlighten, such as art, religion, and philosophy. But resources have always been limited. Life pressures us to compete, whether that competition is over food, territory, desirable mates, or jobs. Individuals compete within their groups over status and position, and groups compete with each other in their quest to dominate. Thus competition is always part of organization even though organizations depend upon cooperation to realize their goals.

Compared to those of other social species like ants, bees, and apes, the complexity of human organizations is enormous. Somewhere along the trajectory from being hunters and gatherers to becoming field hands and farmers, tribes grew into villages, and later into towns, cities, city-states, and nations. Another transformation occurred along with organizational complexity: specialization – the practice of limiting one's activities so that expertise in a specific domain or particular skill can be achieved. For example, your building skills will likely improve if you do not also have to tend fields or educate your children. Of course, other species practice specialization too. Honeybee colonies can number anywhere from 20,000 to 60,000 members, and within them worker bees specialize as nursemaids, guards, construction workers, undertakers, and attendants to the queen.

Specialization serves a society by increasing the quality and variety of goods and services available to its members and by providing efficiencies in their production and delivery that allow more work

3

to be done with less time or effort. As communal life develops through specialization and the interdependence it creates, human society and its organizations become differentiated – different people adopt different roles, and different types of organization are created as people with similar talents and interests work together on specialized tasks. Further encouragement for specialization and differentiation comes from interaction between societies. Some of this interaction involves warfare, but in peaceful times often produces exchange relationships that grow into economies.

Economies depend on trust between people. This trust in turn depends upon experiences of stable, successful exchange. To appreciate what this means in organizational terms requires another concept: institution – a time-honored activity or organization that addresses what would otherwise be a persistent social problem by encouraging behavior that stabilizes society.

Examples of institutions include the handshake, money, banking, marriage, the family, religion, and government. Take the institutions of money and banking. Both were created to address the persistent problem of developing enough trust in trade to create an economy and keep it stable. People make rules about handling money that establish organizational institutions like banks, and other institutions (such as courts and prisons) to handle those who violate the rules.

As institutions stabilized societies and relationships between them developed into differentiated city-states and nations, trade and other organized activities came under formal control through institutional practices such as tax collection and the licensing of organizations. Licensing, or chartering, involves giving organizations legal status as entities along with the right to engage in specified activities (such as trade, industry, law, education).

Over time, institutionalized businesses partnered with churches and armies, combining their wealth and influence to engage in exploration and exploitation. Exploration and the new trade it brought permitted local economies to grow while the potential for exploitation forged competitive relationships between businesses and societies. As this was going on, businesses were discovering new ways to differentiate using technology derived from the invention of the machine.

The invention of machines to do work led to industrialization. Factories that demanded the labor of many were built to house machines and their operators, and to help owners and supervisors manage work. Workers came from rural areas to take advantage of new opportunities to make a living. Cities grew dramatically as industrialization concentrated the populations of the most economically aggressive nations and provided enormous wealth to those with the means to control the largest organizations. Many people moved from farms to cities, and urban values replaced rural ones in the identities of industrialized nations.

Concentrated populations have encouraged the development of service economies that, when combined with the computer, produce another societal transformation of at least the same magnitude brought by the change from agriculture to industry. The computer magnifies the organizational effects of this transition because computer technology, along with the ability to easily traverse the globe, allows some economically powerful organizations to grow larger than many countries. Their growth has promoted capitalism around the world, led by giants like IBM, McDonalds, ABB, Siemens, Sony, and Unilever, supported by the political alignments of capitalist countries.

The trade in which massive business organizations engage has contributed greatly to globalization, which in turn affects cultures and societies by mixing and blending their members as they travel around the world. These changes bring opportunities to further increase the complexity of organizations, though limits to their growth are becoming more and more apparent. For example, the increasing power of corporations in a globalizing economy has put the natural resources of the planet under strain.

Until recently, businesses were governed mainly by their owners, called capitalists because they provide the wealth (i.e. capital) needed to supply the resources business organizations depend upon for their survival. However, a different form of corporate governance is emerging. Known as the stakeholder perspective, this view, as articulated by philosopher R. Edward Freeman (1951– ), holds that anyone whose life is affected by the activities of an organization has a stake in that organization, and thus a right to influence its decisions and actions.

The term 'stakeholder' refers to customers, employees, and owners (shareholders), but also to unions, government regulators, local communities, NGOs, and activists, as well as to the suppliers, distributors, and other partners who make up the supply chain. A supply chain links business organizations that extract and supply raw materials to those that use these materials to make products and distribute them to end-users. The definition of organization expands considerably when it includes the interests of all these stakeholders.

Some believe that including all stakeholders in the definition of an organization creates a democratizing force that replaces hierarchy with more collaborative organizational forms (e.g. networks) and values environmental sustainability and social responsibility as much as profit. The movement to get companies to report on their social responsibility and environmental impact as well as their profit – collectively known as the triple bottom line – is one effect of stakeholder influence. That brand and reputation are becoming as important to organizations as products and profitability is an indication of the growing influence stakeholders exercise.

Some take a dark view of capitalism and its effects. They say that capitalism manufactures the need to buy in order to keep itself and the growth it feeds alive. Once consumerism dominates a society, they warn, it enslaves all.

The argument that capitalism shifts economic activity away from production and toward consumption is supported by the economies of the United States and Western Europe, whose industries have outsourced much of their manufacturing activity to the BRIC countries – Brazil, Russia, India, and China – generating a new phase of economic development. But the political systems and cultures of the BRIC countries are markedly different from those of the United States and Western Europe, and, while their economies are growing rapidly now, questions of stability and sustainability make their long-term influence on the world and its organizations hard to predict.

This short history introduced some of the most enduring ideas associated with organizations: cooperation, competition, goals, growth, size, complexity, differentiation, specialization, economy, globalization, structure, power, institution, and culture. With these ideas in mind, it is time to examine the concept of organizations and its close associates, organization and organizing.

## The three Os: organization, organizations, organizing

It is difficult to say when humans first recognized organization as such, but at some point the idea appeared as an abstract concept. It takes disciplined imagination to think about organization. You can experience the discipline by challenging yourself to make distinctions between three related words we have been using without definition: organization, organizations, and organizing – let's call them the three Os.

Organization and organizations are nouns, while organizing refers to action and thus to a verb. Nouns name things, for example they can refer to entities, states, or conditions, as they do in the terms organizations and organization. Verbs, on the other hand, can be inflected to indicate past, present, and future, bringing with them concern for the effects of passing time.

Organization and organizations (the two nouns) may be more closely related than either is to organizing, but the fact that all three build on the Greek root ὄργανον (*organon*, meaning tool) suggests that the three Os are going to be difficult to distinguish. It is worth the effort, however, as much of what we know about our subject is built on taking one or another of these nuanced distinctions as primary. An analogy to some basic issues in physics may help, since much organizational knowledge derives from insight provided by the physical sciences.

The duality principle in physics states that, depending upon how you observe it, matter can appear as either a particle or a wave. Something similar can be said about organizations. Taking the particle view, you can locate an organization as an entity in time and space. The wave view gives you a sense of organizations as patterns of activity that recur with regularity in a wavelike fashion. The organizational entity known as Oxford University can be found in a set of buildings located in Oxford, England, but taking the wave view, its organization can be seen in recurring teaching and learning activities, term after term.

The two nouns organization and organizations are interrelated in a circular way. When organizational activities (e.g. teaching and learning) are repeated, like the frequencies that recur to form a wave, they come to be thought of as entities or objects. You might call an entity arising from patterns of teaching and learning an educational institution and exemplify it using particular organizations, like Oxford University. When you do this conversion in your mind, you make practices associated

8

with a way of being (acts of organiza*tion*) into entities (organization*s*) in the same way that a wave becomes a particle for physicists.

Conversely, you make a conversion similar to the one that turns a particle into a wave when you consider what is organizational about a particular entity; you think about coordinated practices that lead to desired end states (e.g. teaching and learning leading to education). These ideas are like the two sides of a coin; you cannot view both at the same time, but you cannot have one without the other.

Another definitional challenge arises when you compare organiza*tion(s)* with organiz*ing*. In physics, the Heisenberg uncertainty principle states that you cannot know with equal certainty a particle's position and velocity; the more you know about where it is, the less you can know about where it is going. It is easy to remember the uncertainty principle if you think about an old joke in which Heisenberg gets pulled over by a policeman while driving down the highway. The policeman gets out of his car and walks towards Heisenberg's, motioning for him to lower his window. The policeman says, 'Do you know how fast you were driving, sir?' to which Heisenberg replies, 'No, but I know exactly where I am!'

Like Heisenberg's uncertainty principle, you can think about organization as either outcome or process, but it is tough to think both ways at once. You have to be present in the moment to experience organiz*ing*, whereas you can observe organiza*tion(s)* after the fact of their becoming. Yet, like the impossibility of knowing both a particle's position and velocity, we are likely never to reconcile knowledge of organiza*tion(s)* with that of organiz*ing*.

Notice that I just collapsed organization and organizations into the composite organiza*tion(s)*. Organiza*tion(s)* refers to both

|  | Being | Becoming |
|---|---|---|
| **Abstract** | Organization<br>(an entity)<br><br>'Organization is an arrangement of things, people, ideas and/or activities' | Organization<br>(the act of organizing)<br><br>'Most things improve with more organization' |
| **Concrete** | Organizations<br>(specific cases)<br><br>'IBM, the Red Cross and your family are organizations.' | Organizing<br>(a process)<br><br>'Let's start organizing this mess!' |

2. Some ways to think about differences between the three Os: organization, organizations, and organizing

organization and organizations as outcomes or entities. They are already accomplished states of being. Organiz*ing* (including acts of organization) is an ongoing accomplishment, that is, a process of becoming rather than a state of being.

Even though the three Os cannot substitute for one another, they are intimately related. Organizing processes give rise to acts of organization that, in turn, produce organizations that enable and constrain further organizing processes, and so on. This is the reason we have one basic idea (cooperating to achieve shared goals within a competitive environment) and three interrelated concepts – organization, organizations, and organizing: the three Os.

If you want to focus on the outcomes of organizing, you can specify either particular organizations – entities like Lufthansa or El Al – or characteristics, such as hierarchy or division of labor. If you desire a dynamic understanding of organiz*ing* you must focus on the processes from which organization(s) emerge (e.g. those producing structures or culture) or practices such as those that constitute an airline (e.g. maintaining aircraft, piloting, transporting passengers, and handling baggage).

Historically, managers and organizational researchers favored outcome-based definitions because these lend themselves to objective measurement and thereby support management control. However, as both organization(s) and organizing become more complex in the wake of globalization and technological change, process knowledge becomes increasingly important. If complexity makes it impossible to fully describe an organization or predict the outcomes of organized activity with certainty, you can at least increase your odds of success by improving organizing processes.

We know from comparisons of successful and unsuccessful organizations that formulating strategic vision motivates goal achievement, as does structuring roles and relationships to aid the implementation of strategy. Furthermore, the use of technology can enhance productivity, and culture communicates how things 'really' get done. The supportive design of the physical environment of work also contributes to success. Some of this knowledge is based in an outcome-oriented view, some is process-based, and some mixes the two.

## Metaphors for organization

Metaphor is a way to stimulate imagination for new ideas. Management scholar Gareth Morgan (1943– ) showed that four metaphors in particular have proven their worth helping people to form images of organization: the machine, organism (or living system), culture, and psychic prison. The machine and organism metaphors came first and lend themselves best to visualizing organization(s) as static structures or systems to be designed and controlled either by managers or the environment. The metaphors of culture and psychic prison developed later. Culture presents an image better suited to understanding organizing as a process arising from social interaction and sensemaking, while the psychic prison metaphor offers a critical stance toward the other three. Taken together the four metaphors mark out the same territory covered by the three Os, but add lots of color and texture.

Metaphors work by suggesting similarities between their vehicle (e.g. machine, organism, culture, prison) and its target (in this case, the three Os), but they do so on an aesthetic rather than a rational basis, which is why metaphor complements scientific explanation. So do not think you have to choose between art and science, instead try to appreciate both ways of knowing. It may at first feel strange to think in such different ways, but stretching your mind should help you embrace the complexity and paradox (e.g. cooperation *and* competition) that coming to terms with the three Os requires.

## Organizations as machines

The machine metaphor traces its origins back over 300 years to the start of the industrial age. A machine is designed to effectively perform work of a repetitive nature. In creating scientific management, for example, Frederick Taylor (1856–1915), an engineer, was inspired by his knowledge of how machines work to find the most efficient motions for humans to use when performing manual labor. He then claimed his scientific approach to management dramatically increased industrial labor productivity, an idea later extended to other types of work. Nowadays, the machine metaphor encourages managers to design all aspects of their organizations to maximize efficiency.

In order to design a machine to do work, one must specify a task (e.g. driving nails, weaving cloth). This is as true for organizations as it is for machines. However, the task of an organization is more comprehensive than that of a machine. The organization's purpose, mission, and goals define its task; in other words, its task is roughly equal to its function within society. For a business, this function might be to produce airplanes (Airbus), prepare food (McDonald's), or provide management consulting services (McKinsey & Company). Non-business organizations have purposes and goals too, for example to provide higher education (Oxford University) or protect a community (your local police department).

The machine metaphor promotes the belief that organizations can be engineered to maximize their contribution and minimize their costs to society. Think of the idea of engineering automobiles. As a customer, you hope that the company that manufactures your vehicle will do so in a way that keeps the final cost to you down while also making sure that the car you drive is safe and suffers as few breakdowns as possible. Such a company's task is to design, build, deliver, and service a quality automotive product at a price you can afford. It is the manager's job is to see that this happens efficiently and effectively, and without unnecessarily harming people or the environment, by organizing resources and the work done with them.

Applications of the machine metaphor tend to focus attention on the internal workings of organizations – how they perform core manufacturing or service-delivery tasks. This is the most fitting application of the machine metaphor. But organizations must perform many other tasks, such as purchasing raw materials, selling products and services, and adapting to changes in the environment. Managers too do more than supervise employees, they must also recruit and retain them, design their jobs, and formulate and implement a vision to lead them. The machine metaphor is less well suited to describing these tasks.

Even though most managers are attracted to the idea of treating employees like parts of a well-oiled machine, the human element requires more nuance to be effectively managed. Furthermore, it can be dangerous to ignore what economists call externalities, namely the environment upon which organizations depend for the resources to do their work. Externalities impose constraints that give others power over organizations, and this means organizations must develop and maintain relationships with external agents if they are to survive and prosper. In this they are more like living systems or organisms than machines.

## Organizations as organisms (living systems)

The organism metaphor developed later than that of the machine, emerging along with evolutionary biology, particularly from notions such as the survival of the fittest promoted by Charles Darwin (1809–82). An organism is a living system that depends for survival on its ability to adapt to the environment. Treating organizations as adaptive organisms directs attention to the dynamics of competition, to dependence on resources provided by the environment, and to demands for continual change. Along with the organism metaphor came ideas such as variation, selection, and retention that help explain success and failure rates within populations of organizations. So, too, did the idea that organizations, like organisms, have interrelated parts, an insight no doubt inspired by the practice of dissection in biology research.

By the end of World War II, when the organism metaphor appeared, it had become popular to think that all the sciences were interrelated and that discovery of a unified theory of everything was imminent. The related idea of systems also became influential. A system is anything comprised of parts (subsystems) whose interrelationships produce a level of order and function (the system) that transcends the sum of the parts. In other words, a system has properties that cannot be fully known by examining its parts in isolation. For example, you can dissect a human body but you will not be able to isolate thought or identity, these are emergent properties explained by interactions among the parts, and between the whole and its environment.

The key contribution of systems theory was the idea that different system levels are nested. All systems exist within higher-order systems existing within still more complex systems. According to general systems theory, the name given to this idea by biologist

Ludwig von Bertalanffy (1901–72), each higher-order system includes all the levels beneath or within it.

Kenneth Boulding (1910–93) developed Bertalanffy's ideas into a hierarchy of systems (see Figure 3) with frameworks being the

| Level | Characteristics | Examples |
|---|---|---|
| 1. Framework | • labels and terminology<br>• classification systems | anatomies, geographies<br>lists, indexes, catalogs |
| 2. Clockwork | • cyclical events<br>• simple with regular (or regulated) motions<br>• equilibria or states of balance | solar system<br>simple machines (clock or pulley)<br>equilibrium system of economics |
| 3. Control | • self-control<br>• feedback<br>• transmission of information | thermostat<br>homeostasis<br>auto pilot |
| 4. Open (living) | • self-maintenance<br>• throughput of material<br>• energy input<br>• reproduction | cell<br>river<br>flame |
| 5. Genetic | • division of labor (cells)<br>• differentiated and mutually dependent parts<br>• growth follows 'blue-print' | plant |
| 6. Animal | • mobility<br>• self-awareness<br>• specialized sensory receptors<br>• highly developed nervous system<br>• knowledge structures (image) | dog<br>cat<br>elephant<br>whale or dolphin |
| 7. Human | • self-consciousness<br>• capacity to produce, absorb, and interpret symbols<br>• sense of passing time | you<br>me |
| 8. Social organization | • value system<br>• meaning | businesses<br>governments |
| 9. Transcendental | • 'inescapable unknowables' | metaphysics, aesthetics |

3. The nine levels of general systems theory (GST) tell us that everything can be described as a system composed of lower-order subsystems and that each system is itself part of a higher-order system. Each system level has properties unique to its position in this hierarchy, and a system at any particular level contains lower-order systems such that their properties also apply to the higher order, in cumulative fashion

simplest systems, followed by clockworks, open systems, living systems, humans, social organizations, and something metaphysical that transcends and includes them all. Since organizations contain many lower-level systems, any knowledge about lower levels also applies to them. Hence the aptness of using, for example, biological principles derived from studying living systems to explain the three Os.

A human system contains digestive, anatomical, circulatory, respiratory, and nervous subsystems all serving different functions, such as to take in and convert food to energy, support the weight of the organism and allow it to move around in its environment, transfer oxygen from the lungs to the blood and thereby to the cells throughout the body, and sense the environment so as to respond in adaptive ways. Similarly, the operational core of the organization produces goods and services while staff in finance, marketing, accounting, human resources, communication, and strategy departments perform other functions.

Just as the subsystems of the human body produce the conditions for a human being to emerge but do not account for all that a person is, so the parts of the organization cannot explain a whole organization. Recognition of one of the emergent properties of an organization – its culture – introduces a third metaphor.

## Organizations as cultures

Imagining organizations as machines or as organisms that are living systems relies upon metaphors drawn from the natural sciences, particularly physics and biology. Using culture to imagine the three Os taps the social sciences and humanities.

Anthropology and literature informed those inclined to see organizations as cultures. Cultural anthropologist Clifford Geertz (1926–2006) combined these in offering a symbolic view of culture. Humanistic ways of understanding bring with them new questions, for instance: what social and emotional forces derive from belonging to a group, and how do they influence an organization's structure or the ways in which technology is used? What do concepts like artifact, value, custom, and tradition tell us about organizations? Can culture explain the success some organizations enjoy or the failures of others? What do organizations mean, and how do they produce and influence the meanings they are given?

Many believe that the low-cost carrier Southwest Airlines became successful because its co-founder Herb Kelleher (1931– ) appreciated organizational culture. Kelleher believed that loyal employees would give his airline distinctiveness and competitive advantage in an industry known for cut-throat competition and poor customer service. He also knew that the market for transportation was not being fully served – there was room for a low-cost airline that provided people with an attractive alternative to short- and medium-distance bus, train, and automobile trips. The culture of the airline that Kelleher created to fill this void was built on having fun delivering great service in what was then a stodgy and highly militaristic industry.

The culture metaphor asks you to imagine Kelleher as the chief of an ancient tribe that worships him like a god and follows his lead in everything they do. It is a tribe with unique customs and rituals that maintains its integrity even under extreme external pressure, such as deep economic recession. For example, Kelleher partied hard and long with his employees, often flying to visit them where they worked and then working and playing alongside them. This custom promoted extreme loyalty and also gave him first-hand knowledge of the problems and opportunities his employees faced.

When times were tough, Southwest's employees were known to give back some of their pay when they felt the company needed it to survive. Attachments like these are hard to explain using the machine or living systems metaphors. It takes the emotional and aesthetic nuance of cultural understanding to grasp what is at work in cases like Southwest and other companies that benefit from having beloved organizational cultures.

The culture metaphor emphasizes emotions and values that create a solid and lasting foundation for the activities and aspirations of organizational members. Heroes who personify cultural expectations help people understand what they should do as they engage in everyday life and face the trials and tribulations of the workplace. The ceremonies and rituals that memorialize people and their exploits bind organizational members together, even as telling their stories of the past instructs behavior in the here and now. Taken together, these and other symbols form patterns of meaning that make a culture distinctive and help people identify with one another and honor what they share.

Communicating with symbols and leaving artifact trails allows members to transfer their culture to the next generation, creating continuity across time. But although culture provides stability, it also offers continuity in the face of unavoidable or irresistible change. It takes the confidence of knowing who you are to face a threatening environment or new opportunities that demand taking risk.

There is a darker side to culture. A culture exerts a considerable controlling force over the hearts and minds of its members, who exchange some of their independence for the gift of belonging. If an organization's culture falls under the spell of its top management subculture, members may come to be imprisoned by norms and expectations that do not express their true values and fulfill desires other than their own.

Philosopher Friedrich Engels (1820–95), with whom Karl Marx (1818–83) wrote *The Communist Manifesto*, described this situation as false consciousness, that is, the acceptance of an ideology that conceals realities of subordination, domination, and exploitation. One such ideology involves accepting as normal and necessary the domination hidden within hierarchical relationships. Recognizing hierarchy as a form of domination exposes the prison-like character of hierarchical organizations, suggesting a fourth metaphor – the psychic prison.

## Organizations as psychic prisons

Culture and the unconscious can be regarded as opposite sides of the same coin. Psychiatrist Sigmund Freud (1856–1939) considered culture a collective phenomenon arising from the unconscious dynamics of its members. Carl Jung's (1875–1961) idea of the collective unconscious took the opposing view that our cultural past provides a reservoir of experiences and memories that we tap as our psyches develop. Either way, connecting culture with the unconscious provides a novel way to think about the three Os. For example, Freud's psychoanalysis suggests that emotions such as anxiety and desire produce the realities humans inhabit and thus become part of their organizations.

Freud believed that to live in harmony with others, humans control their impulses through unconscious psychological mechanisms of denial, displacement, projection, rationalization, regression, and sublimation. By helping an individual recognize their emotional impulses and the psychological mechanisms they use to control them, Freud claimed he could rid a patient of neuroses such as depression, hypochondria, obsession, or narcissism.

Organizations have similarly neurotic tendencies that can manifest as debilitating conflict or other dysfunctional collective behavior that threatens their wellbeing. One implication of extending the idea of the unconscious to organizations involves providing therapy to uncover unconscious motives or relieve organizational anxiety and stress. Seen in this way, the metaphor of the unconscious provides a route to organizational self-knowledge and its psychological benefits, including the capacity to alter an organization's personality or identity.

But when they shape an individual's consciousness through collective manifestations of greed, fear, and other negative psychological states associated with domination, organizations become psychic prisons. For instance, repressing or denying the emotions that accompany hierarchical subordination creates oppressive conditions inside employees' minds. Instead of treating whole organizations as patients, as suggested by the metaphor of organizational neurosis, use of the psychic prison metaphor is typically intended to emancipate employees from the bonds of anxiety and desire that prevent them from seeing the harm organizations do to them.

For some, modern capitalism is responsible for the dehumanization and exploitation described by the psychic prison metaphor. They focus on how our personalities, beliefs, tastes, and preferences develop within contexts of mass production and consumption characteristic of Western capitalism. To strengthen their point, they may stress the destructive influence of capitalist organizations on nature, society, and the underprivileged.

For example, the environmental sustainability movement challenges old expectations about the costs an organization should bear, arguing in favor of new rules such as a carbon emissions tax to cover the costs of cleaning up industrial waste and pollution. Similarly, social responsibility advocates pressure organizations to pay a living wage to those who work for them, including employees of subcontractors, and to provide their workers with safe and healthy work environments. Some even suggest that organizations take responsibility for those who live in poverty worldwide on the grounds that the poor pay a price for the wealth the rest enjoy.

Applying the metaphor of a psychic prison raises questions about how organizations might bring about positive change for workers and society, such as freedom, diversity, and respect for our planet and all the forms of life that it nourishes. Portraying the organization as a psychic prison encourages criticism of mainstream management and is intended to awaken our consciousness in the hope of changing organizations for the betterment of the world and all its inhabitants.

# Chapter 2
# What is the best way to organize?

In addition to metaphors, there are two common means of visualizing organizations; both depict structural features. First, you can look at an organization's buildings, their orientation to one another, and the landscape surrounding them. Paying a visit to Google Earth offers an overview of a complex of buildings, such as those of Google's own Googleplex in Mountain View, California, shown in Figure 4. You can also look at architectural elevations and floor plans. Such images tell you much about the physical shapes organizations take and the places they occupy.

A second way to visualize an organization is to draw an organigram, a clever name combining the idea of an organization chart with a diagram. Organigrams depict people and the positions they hold within an organization, typically showing jobs grouped into departments. Each position and/or department is drawn within a box, and each box is linked to other boxes by lines, as shown in Figure 5. Vertical lines represent reporting relationships connecting all the different levels of the organization from top to bottom. Horizontal lines show lateral relationships between those working at the same level of the organization which, when dotted, depict liaison or other coordination roles.

The organigram represents an organization's social structure, while photographs and architectural drawings show aspects of its

4. The roofs of the Googleplex carry 9,000 solar panels, while inside every employee must be located within a few feet of free food by corporate policy

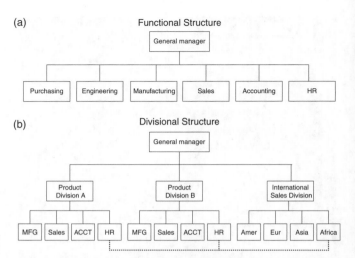

(a) Functional Structure

General manager

| Purchasing | Engineering | Manufacturing | Sales | Accounting | HR |

(b) Divisional Structure

General manager

| Product Division A | Product Division B | International Sales Division |

| MFG | Sales | ACCT | HR | MFG | Sales | ACCT | HR | Amer | Eur | Asia | Africa |

5. Two organization charts: a) shows a functional structure so called because the units represent specialized activities broken into 'functions' such as marketing, HR, and finance; and b) a divisional structure whose (usually much larger) operational units or 'divisions' may or may not be functionally organized

physical structure. Social and physical structures are part of every organization whether or not they are deliberately designed. When they are left to develop on their own, these structures emerge out of the more or less self-managed activities of organizational members as they interact with each other and their physical surroundings. When designed deliberately, they are typically implemented by managers supported by staff specialists in finance, accounting, HR (human resources), marketing, and communication.

Organizational design begins by considering the purpose of organizing and the organization's strategy. Purpose and strategy, in turn, inform decisions about the organization's products and services and the ways in which production and delivery goals will be met. Production and service delivery methods define an organization's technology. Since technology is the means of delivering the organization's output, on which its survival depends, organization designers try to understand how the organization's technical core operates in order to design an efficient and effective organizational structure to support it.

In designing organizational structures, designers also need to consider the environment. An organization's environment controls the resources required to operate the technical core, so organizations adapt to the demands of their environments in order to manage their resource dependencies. The need to support and protect the technical core means that organizational structures must also conform to or fit the environment. But since environments are composed of organizations that constantly adapt in order to stay competitive, environments also change. An organization's design should therefore reflect the amount and frequency of adaptation required to retain organization–environment 'fit.'

Organization designers use strategy, technology, and knowledge about the environment to indicate the form their organization should take, but since size multiplies organizing challenges, size also plays a role in structuring organizations. As the old saying goes, size matters. This phrase is particularly germane to organizations because growth beyond a certain size brings bureaucracy as well as increased influence over other organizations and sometimes the environment itself.

## Organizational social structure and design

Organizational social structure is created by patterns of interaction and relationship through which the work of an organization is accomplished and its purpose realized. Organizations are structured by relationships that grow from interactions, the repetition of which (e.g. in organizational routines) provides stability and helps to ensure cooperation.

In the most general terms, organizational design concerns creating structures that maximize organizational performance in order to be efficient and effective in achieving organizational goals, while minimizing the need to use scarce resources. But designers can get bogged down in their search for the 'right' answers to myriad structural questions.

For example: how should we distribute the authority to establish goals and direct activities toward achieving them? Should we keep our structure integrated by forming one big group to work toward our goals shoulder to shoulder, or should we differentiate tasks by breaking work into its components assigning the pieces to subgroups? Should work be specialized so that trained workers perform a smaller repertoire of tasks more expertly? If we use subgroups, how large should they be such that the span of control of a single manager does not overwhelm her or him? Should all decisions be made at the top (centralized) or should authority be delegated (de-centralized)?

Although these are interesting and important considerations, designing the right organization structures demands deeper understanding of what organization structure is and how it works. The basic idea most organizational designers use is that a structure is effective if it focuses the attention of employees on the activities for which they are responsible, and promotes communication of critical information across the organization. It is efficient if it minimizes the time, effort, capital, and other resource inputs needed to meet goals while maximizing output. This is not as easy as it sounds.

Because it is created from behavior, organizational social structure can never be implemented exactly as designed. Social structures are as much constructed by behavior as the other way around. Furthermore, structure influences strategy as much as strategy influences structure because structure shapes the ways in which strategy is realized in organizational behavior. Strategy, structure, and behavior are mutually influential and interdependent.

What is more, because social structure defines the distribution of organizational power (e.g. the authority to assign tasks and determine reward and promotion opportunities), even the most rational of intentions to design an effective and efficient organization are affected by the desire to control others and the anxiety of being controlled. Sociologist Max Weber (1864–1920) believed that bureaucracy, at least in theory, combats the perversions of unbridled power making room for reasoned choice. Working under this assumption, Weber defined the main components of an organization's social structure: hierarchy, division of labor, and departmentalization.

## Hierarchy

When you first thought about organizations, you might have been tempted to use hierarchy as your sole definition because hierarchy is such a common feature among them. Technically, the term refers to the vertical distribution of authority among organizational positions such that each position is made subordinate to some other. Think of the vertical lines linking the top to the bottom of an organigram.

Vertical lines of authority channel the right to direct and control the activity of others. Authority can be used to make decisions, allocate resources, and reward and punish, so it facilitates the exercise of power. Of course, in addition to this formal authority, there are other sources of power people use in organizations, such as expertise, personal influence, charisma, control over information, or access to powerful others.

Organizational hierarchy creates an authoritative command and control structure through which goals cascade from top to bottom, allowing leaders to give direction to all organizational activity. It also defines the scope of each employee's decision-making authority by indicating when an employee can make their own decisions and when they need to seek approval from the boss. While the distribution of authority to direct activity defines the command part of the command-and-control structure, the control part involves using authority to make and enforce the rules governing behavior.

The same structure that channels authority from top to bottom, channels information from bottom to top. Information flow permits monitoring organizational and individual performance, and authority permits the sanctioning of any infractions committed by those who do not meet performance expectations. The delegated power to reward and punish those beneath a given position in the hierarchy gives formal authority its teeth.

Many people believe that hierarchy is a fundamental aspect of life. After all, social life appears to be hierarchically organized throughout much of the animal kingdom. If you watch a group of male rams interact during mating season, you are likely to observe a fair amount of head-butting, and the strongest male lion eats the most food after a kill (or after feeding his cubs if he is a new father). An organizational hierarchy is, according to this view, supported by natural law.

Sometimes hierarchy's 'natural order' is used to argue that human forms of aggression are 'natural.' However, throughout the animal kingdom, hierarchy is as much about promoting harmony as it is about dominance. Close observation of gray wolves, for example, suggests that the dominant pair in a wolf pack, known as the alphas, assign responsibilities, reinforce roles, and decide where the pack will sleep, what it will hunt, and how to react to approaching animals.

Interestingly, the hierarchical order in a wolf pack is far more likely to be aggressively defended by wolves held in captivity than in the wild. Could human organizations fitting the metaphor of the psychic prison simulate the effect of captivity on wolf packs? It is hard to know without more study, but one thing seems certain, hierarchical status is aggressively defended in most human organizations, mainly through the mechanisms of competition among dominant members (the alphas) of these human packs.

## Division of labor

In a complex society, no one is self-sufficient; there are simply too many tasks to perform for one person to master all. Division of labor provides a solution and it has been around since at least Neolithic times, when evidence shows early hominids performing differentiated roles such as warrior, forager, chief, and shaman. In *The Republic*, the ancient Greek philosopher Plato (c. 427–347 BC) referred to the division of labor when he mused about the fulfillment of a society's needs: 'Well then, how will our state supply these needs? It will need a farmer, a builder, and a weaver, and also, I think, a shoemaker and one or two others to provide for our bodily needs.' He overlooked the roles women and slaves held such as cooking, cleaning, and tending children, though of course these too sustain society.

Trades eventually integrated into organizations, such as within the Dutch shipbuilding industry, where workers who specialized in building only one part of a ship worked under a master shipbuilder. But it was the economist Adam Smith (1723–90) who first explained the importance of the division of labor for industrial society. In his 1776 book *An Inquiry into the Nature and Causes of the Wealth of Nations*, Smith explained that concentrating workers on subtasks to refine their skills allows a group to minimize its costs and maximize its productivity, thereby producing greater wealth. Let me illustrate with a personal anecdote.

An artist who came to me for advice some years ago had been commissioned to make twelve stained-glass windows for a church. It was a much bigger order than she had ever filled before, and she asked me to help her organize her workers to make the windows in the short amount of time she had to complete the job. She had never heard of the division of labor, but when I told her about it, she agreed to give it a try.

She divided the job into subtasks such as making the window frames, cutting and placing the colored glass inside the frames, connecting the glass with lead, and welding the lead together. She designed the windows and managed the glass cutting and assembly, pitching in whenever anyone had trouble with their job, thereby ensuring the quality of the product. When they finished, she told me she was amazed by how much faster the work progressed than it would have if workers had assembled entire windows individually. But she also confessed that nobody had as much fun doing the work or as great a sense of accomplishment at its conclusion.

Organizations pay a human price for treating people like machines, and over the course of history, the effects of the division of labor have met many critics. Adam Smith himself, for example, worried that specialization led to uncreative, ignorant workers disconnected from society, a theme Marx later echoed in his writings on alienation as a consequence of industrialization. Around the same time Marx was writing, naturalist and transcendentalist Henry David Thoreau (1817–62) claimed in *Walden* that disconnection from society caused by the division of labor made the average person in 'civilized' society less wealthy (e.g. in terms of happiness) than one in 'savage' society. This is because 'savages' treat one another as whole persons whereas the 'civilized' act like cogs in a machine.

Those who defend the division of labor accuse critics of romanticizing the pre-industrial past. Even if some must work hard at less than appealing jobs, they reason, everyone now has at least some leisure time thanks to the productivity the division of labor brings.

## Departmentalization

Love it or hate it, most organizations divide their work among employees who each perform a piece of the whole. The division of labor is designed into an organization by defining the scope and scale of task responsibilities for each position in the hierarchy. Different jobs are then grouped according to similarities (a functional structure including departments of marketing, accounting, manufacturing, sales, and so on), or according to the products, type of customer, or geographical region served (a divisional structure). Thus, in addition to defining a hierarchy and specifying a division of labor, organization design involves departmentalizing activities, in other words, finding an effective way to group tasks and jobs.

Matrix structures (Figure 6) provide another way of departmentalizing work that is common in engineering, design, and consulting firms. In a matrix, each worker reports to at least two different managers, one a functional expert who manages everyone with the same functional specialty regardless of their project team assignments, and the other a project manager in charge of everyone assigned to the same project. Since individuals may have a skill useful to more than one project team, they may be assigned to more than one project and thus report to multiple project managers as well as a functional boss.

Starting or ending a project is as simple as assembling or dispersing a team and thus affects only a few people. Therefore, matrix organizations are fast and flexible when compared to other structural types where change involves restructuring the entire organization. For this reason, matrix structures adapt well to rapidly changing environments.

The flexibility of a matrix is well suited to organizations that employ many experts who would be too costly to keep on the payroll were they not fully employed. Because expertise can be

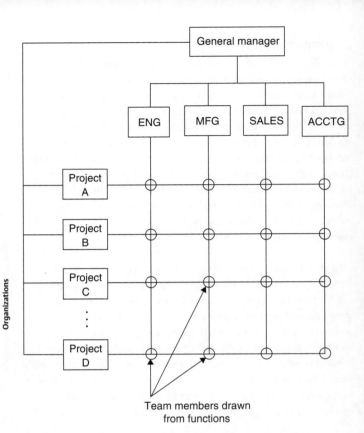

Team members drawn
from functions

**6. A matrix structure allows for greater flexibility than does a
functional or divisional structure because project teams can be formed
and disbanded without restructuring the entire organization**

shared across many temporary work units, the high salaries experts
command can be justified. Moreover, the highly educated
professionals typical of matrix organizations can handle the
greater complexity of working in an organization that requires
them to juggle the demands of multiple managers and
ever-changing work requirements.

## Bureaucracy

Almost every organization develops bureaucracy as it grows. Bureaucracy is characteristic of most governments, nearly every university, established religious orders, and large corporations the world over. According to Weber, it emerged from the Middle Ages as a response to rampant nepotism and other abuses of power occurring throughout feudal societies. Heralded at the time as morally superior to the available alternatives such as fiefdoms, bureaucracy relies upon rationality (e.g. optimizing decisions for the sake of goal achievement) rather than favoritism to govern the fair distribution and use of resources and authority.

Bureaucracy emerges when systems are large, rely upon recognized technical expertise, or continue indefinitely, as government agencies and large businesses often do. It is characterized by a fixed division of labor, a hierarchy of bureaus (e.g. departments, ministries) with their own well-defined spheres of governance, and a set of rules governing performance. Those appointed to work for a bureaucracy are selected on the basis of their technical qualifications and promotions are based on seniority or achievement as determined by superiors operating within the rules of their office. Strict discipline and control is expected throughout.

Ideally, bureaucracy is a system for turning employees of quite average ability into rational decision-makers able to serve their constituencies, clients, or customers with impartiality and efficiency. The bureaucratic form promises reliable decision-making, merit-based selection and promotion, and the impersonal and, therefore, fair application of rules. When organizations are large and operate routine technologies in fairly stable environments, bureaucracy will generally produce these benefits, though not without some negative consequences.

Although Weber was one of the first to promote bureaucracy as an antidote to the feudal structures from which they arose, he was also quite critical of it, referring to the 'polar night of icy darkness' bureaucracy brings to society. As other critics have since noted, bureaucracy defines tasks so narrowly and renders organization so complex that its participants ultimately lose sight of their larger purposes. Regardless of what it was originally designed to do, they say, bureaucracy ultimately only perpetuates itself. Weber declared the fully established bureaucracy as 'among those social structures which are the hardest to destroy,' and he regarded bureaucracy as an 'iron cage' because of its impersonal and dehumanizing nature, for better and worse, 'eliminating from official business love, hatred, and all purely personal, irrational, and emotional elements.'

Because of its many limitations, bureaucracy is decidedly *in*appropriate in many situations. Small organizations do not need bureaucracy; their size makes direct supervision and centralized decision-making easy and natural. In these situations, informal controls are cheap, and since they are more satisfying for organizational members, the codified rules of bureaucracy are unnecessary, they waste time, and de-motivate employees.

Nor can bureaucracy accommodate constant and rapid change. Change requires rewriting policies and rules and disseminating revisions to decision-makers who must then remember them or constantly refer to manuals and memos to implement them properly. Thus, whenever flexibility is a primary consideration, bureaucracy becomes a hindrance. What is more, many people detest bureaucracy, as is indicated by such familiar expressions as 'the bureaucratic run around' and 'red tape.'

Organizations that employ large numbers of professionals will not perform well if they become overly bureaucratic. Professionals are highly trained and socialized to accept high standards of performance so that bureaucratic rules and procedures just get in

34

their way. An organization will not receive full value from its professional employees if it insists that they do only what they are told. Professionals hired for their knowledge and expertise must have the discretion to use their skills and training or much of their value will be wasted. Such waste is inefficient from the point of view of the organization, and frustrating and offensive from the perspective of employees.

The professionalization of management through the Master of Business Administration (MBA) and Master of Public Administration (MPA) degrees has created interesting tensions around bureaucratic values. Professional managers have come into increasing conflict with the inflexibility of bureaucracy. The great wave of privatization that swept capitalist countries in response to the globalization of capital flows brought a shift away from bureaucracy in many societies.

However, the dangers of relinquishing bureaucracy's commitment to fairness and rule-mindedness have been made abundantly clear by recent scandals in the banking sector followed by global recession and the collapse of several national economies. It seems there will always be a tension between the forces for adaptation and those for sticking to what we know works, and we may be wise to tread carefully the line separating too much and too little bureaucracy.

## The physical structure of organizations

For a long time, organization designers believed in the old adage 'form follows function.' But function also follows form, which can be observed in the ways we adapt to a new office or home by reorganizing our belongings and establishing new pathways between locations we visit regularly. As former British prime minister Winston Churchill (1874–1965) once observed: 'We shape our buildings and afterward our buildings shape us.'

Architects know that the design of buildings influences how people move around and use space, and who they meet as they do so. A well-designed organization takes account of the effects of physical structure, but regardless of whether an organization is well designed from a physical standpoint, its physical structure influences how people work and the relationships they form with one another. Because relationships are affected by where we sit and how we like our work environment, physical structure influences social structure.

To repay the favor, social structure has a big say in what spaces organizational members occupy and how much control they have over their allotment – how they decorate it, who gets to enter at will, who can observe them. The most potent example of physical space interacting with social structure comes from British philosopher and social theorist Jeremy Bentham (1748–1832), whose brother designed what Bentham called a Panopticon and described as 'a new principle of construction applicable to any sort of establishment, in which persons of any description are to be kept under inspection.'

In a prison, for example, the Panopticon arranges prison cells in a ring facing a central tower to be occupied by guards who are shielded from view. According to Bentham:

> ...the more constantly the persons to be inspected are under the eyes of the persons who should inspect them, the more perfectly will the purpose of the establishment have been attained. Ideal perfection, if that were the object, would require that each person should actually be in that predicament, during every instant of time. This being impossible, the next thing to be wished for is, that, at every instant, seeing reason to believe as much, and not being able to satisfy himself to the contrary, he should *conceive* himself to be so.

Thinking you might be watched at any time creates pressure to behave as if you are watched all the time. Self-monitoring by the

7. A Panopticon prison, like the design Jeremy Bentham described, has a the central tower surrounded by cells from which wardens can observe prisoners without themselves being observed

prisoners cuts down on the actual monitoring needed and thus on the number of guards required. The Panopticon is thus an efficient device for achieving control, which is why it is a favorite example of those who employ the metaphor of the psychic prison to describe modern organizations. In their terms, the Panopticon establishes 'the Gaze,' the psychic presence of authority that works through self-monitoring to control subjects, whether they are prison inmates, patients in hospitals or psychiatric wards, or workers on assembly lines.

Less ominous, perhaps, but no less powerful, the physical structures of our homes, schools, churches, businesses, and other organizations influence the patterns of activity that take place within them. The walls in your home define the paths you can follow as you move, say from the kitchen to your bedroom, and their thickness determines what you will hear – and overhear. The location of your living and working spaces relative to those of your co-workers determines the likelihood and frequency with which you will informally meet as you go about your daily activities. Proximity of spaces occupied is related to amount of contact, which, in turn, influences your chances of forming working relationships, friendships, and, for some, even who they will marry.

There are many elements of physical structure that affect how various activities are accomplished and how we feel as we engage in them. These elements include buildings and their locales, décor, furniture, equipment, and even human bodies. And don't forget the importance of location. How these elements are arranged forms the physical structure of the organization, and while all of these features can be designed by architects, engineers, and interior designers, they will exist even when no one intentionally designs them.

All organizations, no matter how small, are affected by the design of their physical structure. While large expansive organizations, like global airlines, multinationals, franchises, and retail chains, might superimpose their geographies on a map of a nation or the world, small organizations can draw their geographies on the floor plan of the building they occupy. Within a specific building, the internal placement of objects, especially walls, large pieces of furniture, equipment, and artwork, carve up and help to define the interior spaces of buildings. The assignment of people to specific locations and groups to particular areas within a building is another key aspect of internal layout.

Layout affects the way in which individuals and groups communicate and coordinate their efforts, including formal reporting as well as grapevines and rumor mills. The most obvious example of the relationship between layout and coordination is the assembly line with people and tools located at fixed positions past which the material to be assembled moves. If the layout of an assembly line is well designed, many inefficiencies and inconveniences will be avoided in the production process. But

38

regardless of the technology they use, employees are affected by the distribution and arrangement of the spaces they occupy, so designing physical space to support technology promotes efficiency and effectiveness.

What is more, the relationships people establish with their spaces produce meanings that become part of organizational culture. How they decorate and arrange space allows them to express their values within that culture. Think about how college professors surround themselves with their books and diplomas, or executives with expensive furnishings, fine art, or other symbols of power and achievement. Status is often attributed to those who occupy large, well-appointed offices with attractive views, or to whom parking spaces have been assigned.

Façade, landscaping, furnishings and appointments, the use of color and form, displays of products or technology, and many other features of design and décor contribute to the messages an organization communicates both internally and externally. Design and décor offer a visual language through which employees indicate their status and power to one another, while they offer important clues about the organization's culture and values to the world outside its walls. Take the example of an organization occupying low-rent facilities furnished minimally. Such an organization may communicate its commitment to a low-cost strategy or tell you that it is unaware or unconcerned about its physical appearance or perhaps even about its employees' wellbeing.

Because the physical appearance of an organization is a potent medium in which to create a lasting impression, some managers attempt to influence organizational identity and corporate image by focusing on elements of physical structure. Elements with particular potential to represent organizational identity or to influence corporate image include: dramatic architectural features (façade, roofline, lighting effects, office interiors, decorating themes), product design, logo, corporate literature (e.g. annual reports, brochures), and uniforms or dress codes.

When they are carefully designed to complement each other, these physical design elements influence impressions of organizational credibility and character and can symbolically reinforce strategic vision. Keep in mind, however, that their interpretations, and hence their meanings, are open to other influences than those intended by managers and designers.

## The influence of technology and the environment

Long before humans arrived on the scene, chimpanzees used sticks and rocks to knock food from trees, crush nuts and berries, and dig insects out of the ground. Gorillas have been spotted using tree branches to test the depth of river water. They are using technology, which refers to knowledge-enhanced means of doing something practical with tools.

Knowledge of how to control fire, the invention of the wheel, the printing press, and the computer are all examples of technologies that altered the course of human civilization. Anthropologists trace the first human technology back at least 2.5 million years to the Stone Age, when early hominids used bones and stones to cut, scrap, and pulverize as they foraged for food, butchered dead animals, and tanned hides to make shelter and clothing.

Flint tools are a particularly interesting early technology. They are formed by using stones or bones to chip flakes from a piece of flint, leaving behind an extremely sharp edge. Flint tools show that early humans learned to use one tool (stone or bone) to make others (axes and arrowheads). In their turn, arrowheads were combined with sticks and string made from plant fiber to create arrows and spears. The making and use of flint tools mark the start of a progression of innovation that continues today: the use of one tool suggests and enables the making of other tools with different uses, and so on.

By definition, technology involves tools, machines, and other equipment devised for doing work, and the craft or knowledge it takes to produce and operate them. But the idea of technology also carries associations to human development. In this respect, it can evoke strong and decidedly different emotions, for instance the belief in technologically driven innovation as a means to sustain or improve life, or the opposite – a fear of the ultimate consequences of addiction to technology and its threat to planet Earth.

Technology affects society and the environment in many ways, some good and others not. In many societies, technology develops advanced economy and creates efficiencies that, when combined with the division of labor, allow more leisure time. However, many technological processes are non-sustainable in that they deplete or destroy natural resources. For better and worse, technology influences our values, and technological advances often present ethical questions never faced before, such as deciding who is to receive the benefits of life-saving but expensive new medical technologies, or whether the use of fossil fuels to provide energy should be continued in the face of global warming.

Philosophers Martin Heidegger (1889–1976) and Herbert Marcuse (1898–1979) believed that societies become flawed by their dependence on technological solutions to their problems, leading to the loss of freedom or diminished psychological health rather than promised improvements in living conditions. Heidegger presented such a view in *The Question Concerning Technology*, in which he stated, 'we shall never experience our relationship to the essence of technology so long as we merely conceive and push forward the technological, put up with it, or evade it. Everywhere we remain unfree and chained to technology, whether we passionately affirm or deny it.' Read George Orwell's novel

*Nineteen Eighty-Four*, or watch the Wachowski brothers' film *The Matrix* for similarly dystopian views of technology.

Returning to metaphors, recall how the machine metaphor encouraged us to transfer the idea of efficient energy use from machines to humans, thereby inspiring the psychic prison metaphor. Depending on which metaphor you apply, you will consider what comes next very differently. Many economists, engineers, and managers think of entire organizations as complex tools or machines for production, that is, as technologies a society uses to provide its members with the things that they need and desire. For example, electronics firms are technologies for the design and manufacture of semiconductors and other components assembled into computers, electronic equipment, tools, games, and toys. Hospitals are technologies to care for people who are ill and universities technologies for educating citizens.

Exchanges of the products, services, and information enabled by technology create an economy. In these terms, an economy is powered by a vast sea of organizations whose technologies collectively produce a nation's gross domestic product (GDP) or total output of goods and services. The term 'technology' used in this way refers to the means organizations use to convert raw inputs into finished outputs, and to deliver products and services to customers and clients, as diagrammed in Figure 8.

Depending upon what role an organization plays in society, its technology will differ from that of other kinds of organizations doing different things. Three generic technologies -- mediating, long-linked, and intensive – will give you an idea about how technologies can differ and what these differences mean for the way organizations are socially and physically structured. Each technology brings with it a different way of working, commonly characterized by the type of task interdependence it produces (see Figure 9). Task interdependence, in turn, can be used to predict the amount and type of coordination an organization needs.

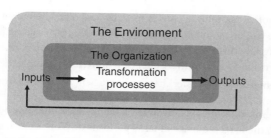

The Environment

The Organization

Inputs → Transformation processes → Outputs

**8. The technology of the organization is connected to the environment by the need for resource inputs and a market for the product and/or service that forms its output**

Mediating technology brings parties to an exchange together (Figure 9a). Bankers use funds provided by savers to make loans to borrowers, real estate agents broker the buying and selling of real estate property, and eBay provides a means for people who want to sell pretty much anything to make an exchange with people who want to buy it. Agents and brokers require limited coordination to do their work, and so an organization built around mediating technology involves little more than pooling the efforts of employees working independently of one another.

Pooled interdependence requires rules and procedures to coordinate the work performed within a mediating technology. The branches of a retail bank, for example, use rules and standard procedures such as those for opening bank accounts, investing in certificates of deposit or mutual funds, and applying for and approving loans and lines of credit. Rules and procedures set standards for how decisions should be made and work processes performed. They contribute to coordination by assuring that desired activities are carried out in an acceptable manner even if they take place in different parts of the world.

Long-linked technology occurs in assembly-line manufacturing (Figure 9b) such as that used to produce automobiles. In automotive assembly, a chassis must be assembled before an engine can be mounted, and so on. Work takes place along a moving line that passes work stations. At each station, a worker performs their task in the sequence required to assemble the finished product.

Long-linked technology involves sequential task interdependence due to the fixed sequence of tasks performed. Work done later

(a)

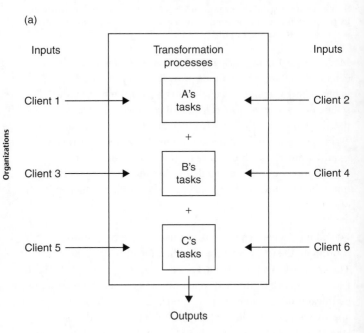

(b)

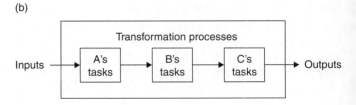

(c)

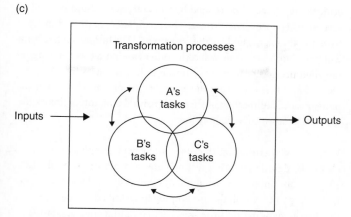

**9. Three technologies: a) mediating, b) long-linked, and c) intensive**

in the sequence suffers when work preceding it is faulty or delayed. To avoid any interruptions in production, coordination through careful planning of tasks and scheduling of workers is imperative. Schedules specify the period of time in which activities are to be accomplished. They also communicate the assignment of individuals to tasks.

The greatest degree of task interdependence – reciprocal – occurs within intensive technologies that require a third form of coordination – mutual adjustment (see Figure 9c). The primary difference between sequential and reciprocal task interdependence is that, where long-linked technologies involve work flows that move in one direction only, the reciprocal work flows of intensive technology generally take the form of teamwork. Intensive technologies require joint decision-making and either physical co-location or a direct and instantaneous channel of communication such as a satellite link.

As a prototypical example of intensive technology with reciprocal task interdependence, think of a patient entering the emergency room of a hospital. First, the patient's status is evaluated. If they are

45

critically ill, they will be treated by a doctor, nurses, and possibly several other specialists at once. The emergency room staff must work in tandem to stabilize the patient, and the tasks each performs will have implications for what the others are doing. When surgery is required, another unit of the hospital that also uses intensive technology takes over from the emergency room, and after that the patient moves to recovery – three intensive technologies linked together in a sort of assembly line.

In fact, any organization that uses intensive technology uses long-linked and mediating technologies as well. In hospitals, ER, surgical, and intensive care units operate using intensive technology; but hospitals also employ long-linked technology during the handing off processes between units, and mediating technology to pool the activities of the healthcare workers with those in the billing department, cafeteria, parking structures, and so forth.

Notice how the hospital example shows the general rule that, as task interdependence increases from pooled to sequential and reciprocal, more mechanisms of coordination are required for effective organization. Pooled interdependence only requires rules and procedures, but sequential interdependence uses rules, procedures, and scheduling, while reciprocal interdependence uses all these forms of coordination plus mutual adjustment, as indicated in Figure 10.

| Type of Technology | Task Interdependence | Coordination Mechanism |
|---|---|---|
| Mediating | Pooled | Rules and procedures |
| Long-linked | Sequential | Schedules |
| Intensive | Reciprocal | Mutual adjustment |

10. As task interdependence increases from pooled to sequential to reciprocal, mechanisms of coordination are added to the organization

When designing organizational structures, it is generally best to begin by planning for any reciprocal task interdependence because this requires the most costly forms of coordination and because problems with needed mutual adjustment are the most likely to produce errors and other inefficiencies. Sequential interdependence is the next most critical to accommodate, followed by pooled interdependence.

## New technology and the computer revolution

The profound changes brought about by computing have produced so-called new technology, an odd label given these technologies have been around for a long time now. The term 'new technology' refers to tools, equipment, and methods of production and service delivery made possibly by advances in electronics, particularly computer chips and satellite communication networks. These technologies have radically transformed work and organizations by reducing the need for physical proximity, and face-to-face coordination. In doing so, they have encouraged virtual organizations and enabled networking.

Structurally speaking, new technologies allow for greater decentralization of decision-making and a reduction of hierarchy because data are more readily available and control can be exercised via software programs accessed electronically from anywhere. Workers find work opportunities posted on internet sites and do their work on their own time, often submitting their output over the internet as well. There is no reason for many workers to ever meet one another or their employer, thus greatly decreasing the number of managers required and flattening the hierarchy while reducing the costs of coordination. Very few people need to be permanently employed in such virtual organizations, and even the few who remain can work from remote locations, such as their homes or while in transit. Organizing remains, but formal organization all but disappears.

As an example, consider txteagle, a 'crowdsourcing' enterprise that taps the abilities of literate people with cell phones who live in developing countries. The company estimates there are currently two billion such people living on less than $5 a day. Using cell phone technology, txteagle commissions them to do text-, audio-, and image-based tasks such as translating short passages of text into their local dialect. These freelance workers use their phones to receive assignments, complete tasks, and mail in their contribution. In exchange for their labor, they receive credit, often only a few cents per job, which is placed into their cell phone account.

As you can see, work changes considerably with the use of new technologies. Workers deal with more information coming from many sources and with software programs, rather than human supervisors, that monitor their performance and correct their errors. But examining the relationships between technology

## HOW IT WORKS

txteagle solves businesses' problems by crowd-sourcing to developing-world mobile phone subscribers

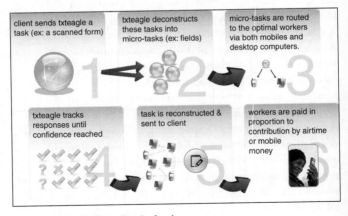

client sends txteagle a task (ex: a scanned form)

txteagle deconstructs these tasks into micro-tasks (ex: fields)

micro-tasks are routed to the optimal workers via both mobiles and desktop computers.

txteagle tracks responses until confidence reached

task is reconstructed & sent to client

workers are paid in proportion to contribution by airtime or mobile money

11. How txteagle describes its business

and the environments and organizational structures that new technologies have altered remains fundamental to addressing questions concerning how best to organize for a particular purpose.

## The technological imperative versus contingency theory: an endless search for the best way to organize

How do technology and environment influence organization? Clearly, there is a connection between the work accomplished using a particular technology and the way workers are organized, as shown by the social structural concepts of task interdependence and coordination. Sociologist Joan Woodward (1916–71) conducted a study in the 1950s that was the first to show the links between technology and social structure.

Woodward's research showed that particular organizational configurations are best suited to different technologies, and many concluded from her study that technology determines structural features like centralization (the concentration of authority at the top of the organization), span of control (how many people report to each boss), and formalization (the extent to which rules and procedures are written down). But this idea, known as the technological imperative, turned out to give an incomplete picture.

Subsequent research provided evidence that the best way to organize depends (is contingent) upon the situation the organization faces both internally (due to its technology) and externally (due to dependence on other organizations and actors in the environment). Known as contingency theory, the new idea promised a formula to determine the best way to organize depending upon the technology in use *and* the environment. It is a little like the board game Cluedo where players try to be the first to determine on the basis of a series of clues who is guilty of a murder, the room in which it occurred, and with what instrument. Instead of Colonel Mustard in the library with a candlestick, contingency theory tries to determine the best organizational structure on the basis of clues about technology and the environment.

Of course, organizational designers face more possibilities than those used in a game of Cluedo. What is more, new contingencies seem always to be presenting themselves, continually adding factors to the list of things that 'determine' organizational structure. Unfortunately, the factors are themselves so complexly interrelated it is unlikely contingency theory will ever define the best match between a given structure, the technology in use, and the environment the organization inhabits.

The trouble is that the abundance of factors that favor a particular structure makes predicting the appropriate organizational design too complex to yield a clear solution. Not to mention the effects of rapid change, which can quickly render any solution out of date. But there is another reason why predicting the best organizational design may be impossible. This explanation requires focusing on meaning.

# Chapter 3
# **What does it mean to be an organization?**

We have already seen that there are many factors to consider when explaining how environments influence organization(s) and organizing. One way of accounting for them is the seven sectors shown in Figure 12. The technological, economic, and physical sectors comprise many objective features of the environment

**12. Sectors of the environment that shape organizing practices and the organizations that emerge from and within them**

whose effects can be measured using methods based in mathematics borrowed from the natural sciences. But the interpretive social sciences – particularly as found in social psychology, organizational sociology, and cultural anthropology – also make important contributions, many relevant to the remaining sectors. These disciplines bring meaning into focus.

Focusing on meaning shows how thoughts, actions, and the way we use language create the organizations we think and talk about when we employ terms such as environment, technology, and structure. To address what and how organizations come to mean what they do requires familiarity with sensemaking and the social construction of reality.

## Social construction and sensemaking

In 1967, cognitive sociologist Harold Garfinkel (1917– ) reported the results of field experiments performed by his students. Garfinkel had instructed the students to violate commonsense expectations, such as how to behave while shopping in a department store or while eating a family dinner. For example, they might bargain over a purchase in a department store, or behave as if they had forgotten the rules of etiquette while dining with family or friends.

Garfinkel's students reported that the experiments caused confusion, discomfort, and sometimes offense, yet although a great deal of nonsense was produced in the process, the prevailing social order never collapsed. Instead, participants redoubled their efforts to maintain things-as-usual. For example, the dining experiment provoked responses like: 'You're just kidding around, right?' and 'Why don't you come back when you can behave like a normal human being?' The experiments showed that people conspire to achieve the taken-for-grantedness of their everyday lives, even if they normally do so unwittingly. The sense everyday life makes, Garfinkel concluded, is a social accomplishment.

Around the same time Garfinkel's students performed their experiments, sociologists Peter Berger (1929– ) and Thomas Luckmann (1927– ) proposed that reality is negotiated and organized by our interpretations of things and events happening around us. They called the process by which we socially shape reality 'social construction.' In their words: 'The primary knowledge [of reality]...is the sum total of "what everybody knows" about a social world, an assemblage of maxims, morals, proverbial nuggets of wisdom, values and beliefs, myths, and so forth.' The interpretive work of social construction occurs as we interact with others and together find out what we are up to. Seen in this light, Garfinkel's students had thrown a wrench in the works of socially constructed reality, thereby revealing some of the social mechanisms we use every day.

Because they construct reality as their members interact, different groups can construct different realities, and the constructions of one period in time may not be the same as those of another. This complicates the notion of socially constructed reality by presenting numerous, and sometimes competing, social constructions that change over time, leaving the impression that socially constructed reality is at best a plurality. But because the processes of social construction work pretty much the same across the board, focusing on how social construction takes place offers a good way to deal with the complexity it produces.

As humans interact, they shape meaning intersubjectively, that is, they negotiate meaning across the private spheres of their individual psyches. Intersubjectivity, the domain of cross-individual (i.e. social) construction, makes reality appear to be external because much of the construction work takes place outside of individual participants' subjective awareness. It is still subjective, but in an interpersonal domain. You might think of intersubjectivity as collective consciousness, in contrast to Jung's notion of the collective unconscious.

None of this implies that socially constructed reality is unreal. As sociologist William Isaac Thomas (1863–1947) put it: 'If men define situations as real they are real in their consequences.' Even if people are wrong about their situations, their beliefs will affect their behavior just the same as if beliefs were objective facts. What is more, the material consequences of behavior *are* objective facts.

Social constructions can be thought of as social facts or facts of life. They do not exist objectively; instead, they appear when we objectify our experiences and talk to each other about them in order to help us make sense of our lives. Objectification is how socially constructed reality differs from what we usually mean by reality. In so-called ordinary reality, we presume that objects exist independently of our thoughts or speech regarding them. By contrast, socially constructed reality is a product of our perceptions, thoughts, feelings, and statements about it, all of which are influenced by social, cultural, legal, and political contexts and by the language we use.

Organizational psychologist Karl Weick (1936– ) contributed to understanding social construction processes when he proposed that humans use sensemaking to give meaning to experience. Sensemaking involves breaking experience into chunks that are then assigned meaning. Weick compared it to mapmaking where a land mass is broken up into various territories constructed by imposing boundaries around them. According to Weick, humans create cognitive maps of particular aspects of their experience to help them find their way around the social world, just as they use maps of the physical world. Of course, for cognitive maps to coordinate behavior effectively there needs to be a fair amount of intersubjective agreement about them.

A cognitive map of socially constructed reality in many ways *is* the territory mapped, which makes it easy to think that something exists objectively when it has been intersubjectively created from sensemaking processes. This applies particularly to organizations, Weick noted, because when a group collectively maps their organizing activities, their cognitive mapping process gives them the sense that an organization exists. For Weick, organizing exists, but organizations do not. In his view, when someone talks about an organization, they refer to a cognitive map, not to an entity in the domain of material objects.

But cognitive maps do have material implications because they affect and are affected by behavior. Weick proposed the term 'enactment' to explain how thought and behavior guided by cognitive maps construct reality, including organizing. He put it like this: 'When people act they unrandomize variables, insert vestiges of orderliness, and literally create their own constraints.' He deliberately chose the term 'en*act*ment' (versus en*think*ment) to emphasize the role behavior plays and to make the point that sensemaking is not *all* in our heads.

Weick used enactment theory to describe how the environment is socially constructed and reconstructed as people define what will be considered information, collect and analyze their data, use it to make decisions, and act. He claimed that: 'They take undefined space, time, and action and draw lines, establish categories, and coin labels that create new features of the environment that did not exist before.'

While organizational members generally assume the environment is objective and collect data to analyze it, their analysis is what actually creates (objectifies) the environment to which they then respond. Their responses construct the environment they set themselves up to expect by confirming and thus further objectifying their reality. To illustrate his point, Weick employed an apocryphal example of a group of lost soldiers using a map of the Pyrenees to find their way out of the Alps. Believing the map represented the terrain in which they were lost helped the soldiers orient themselves and take action. Their action, an enactment of the belief that they possessed a map of the Alps, led them out of danger.

Social construction and sensemaking operate beneath ordinary awareness, but can be intentional and even politically motivated. For example, in the 1960s members of the African American subculture of the United States altered both their collective identity and image by insisting on being referred to as Black rather than Negro. The Black Pride movement that followed advanced their cause and demonstrated the potential of social construction to produce change through enactment.

If continuous processes of social (re)construction, sensemaking, and enactment create stability, then change can occur when altered meaning is symbolized, communicated to, and accepted by others. However, in spite of impressive strides within the black community, including President Barack Obama's election in 2008, much about US race relations remains mired in conservatism. In sensemaking terms, a new reality is still being socially constructed while the old one continues to be re-enacted. How then shall we explain the persistence of social constructions, including those we refer to as organizations? Institutional theory offers one answer.

## Institutions, institutionalization, and the institutional environment

Institutions are powerful influences on behavior and important mechanisms of civilization and society. An institution is a relatively permanent feature of social life associated with behavior so often repeated that few give it a second thought, which is how institutions come to control us without our realizing it. Think of the handshake in Western culture, or a bow in the East. Both practices have been institutionalized in social contexts where participants often perform them out of habit.

The term 'institution' can be confusing in that categories of organization and particular organizations that are permanent fixtures of society are also referred to as institutions. The corporation and IBM are good examples. Thus, the term 'institution' can refer to a practice (the handshake, the bow), a type or category of organization (the corporation, a hospital), or a specific organization (IBM, the Red Cross). What is more, institutionalized myths and logics have also been invoked.

Even more confusion arises from circularity in the definitions of institution and institutionalization. For example, an institution is distinguished from a non-institution by having been institutionalized, and institutionalized ways of thinking (aka institutional myths and logics) are claimed to uphold the practices that create institutions. In spite of these definitional challenges, institutional theory provides much insight into taken-for-granted, socially constructed reality.

## Legitimacy, legitimation, and institutionalized expectations

Institutions and institutionalization processes are important because of the legitimacy they provide. You can think of legitimacy as a social resource in contrast with capital or raw material resources on which organizations also depend. Without legitimacy it is difficult for an organization to thrive because it has to work so hard to justify its existence in the eyes of stakeholders such as regulators, investors, media, and the public. A bank has to look like a bank or people won't trust their money to it. Conversely, online (virtual) universities have to work extra hard to convince prospective students and employers that they are legitimate alternatives to traditional institutions of higher learning.

Institutionalized expectations, such as those defining what is a bank or a university, influence whether or not a particular

57

organization is considered legitimate. And concern for legitimacy prompts organizations to adopt accepted forms and practices without regard for whether or not these address the organization's objective needs. For example, why do we trade faculty positions for investments in fancy new university buildings? Are such choices motivated by rationality or legitimacy? The business practice of couching decisions in the language of data and statistics, regardless of whether this helps or hinders decision-making, is a good example of how pressures for legitimacy (i.e. wanting to appear rational) can triumph over objectivity (being rational).

Legitimation pressures come from three sources: culture, regulation, and desire for success. Cultural expectations produce normative pressure. For example, the expectation that employing professional managers will ensure that organizational decisions are made rationally leads many organizations to hire graduates of MBA or MPA programs, the presence of whom, in turn, reinforces cultural beliefs in professionalism and rational decision-making. Regulation produces coercive pressure, such as the felt need to comply with laws and regulations enforced by negative sanctions like fines or imprisonment. The desire to copy the success of others produces mimetic pressure exemplified by benchmarking, a modern management practice wherein management teams study widely admired organizations in the hope of inspiring new success back home.

It is easy to see the value of legitimacy to organizations that have lost it. ENRON and Arthur Anderson, once admired and emulated US corporations, were put out of business practically overnight by normative sanctions (e.g. loss of the public's trust) and subsequent coercive legal action when these organizations conspired to cover up major fraud perpetrated by ENRON. While losses of legitimacy are rarely this dramatic, its importance should never be underestimated. Like the raw materials essential to manufacturing technologies, legitimacy keeps organizations operational. But unlike raw material such as steel, legitimacy is created by human sensemaking as it occurs in and around organizations, forming the institutional environment.

## Institutional environments: the role of markets, bureaucracies, and social movements

The institutional environment appears because institutions become mutually dependent and intertwined, creating a complex web of mutually enacting social constructions. This means that, as institutions, organizations are embedded within a larger institutional order comprised of the cultural, social, political, and legal sectors of the environment. Organizational structures and practices reflect as well as respond to rules, laws, and conventions built into the institutional environment that controls them even though they may not be fully aware of these effects.

Two of the most powerful forces of the institutional environment are markets and hierarchies. Of course, when we think of markets, we think of trade and business. However, although they are not technically under the influence of market forces, public sector organizations often simulate them by setting up internal conditions that mimic competition in order to put pressure on managers to cut costs (an effect of mimetic pressure to adopt successful corporate practices). A market creates economic competition through which prices and profits regulate the behavior of member organizations with minimal intervention – what Adam Smith called the 'invisible hand.'

The invisible hand of the market makes sure that organizations do not unfairly exploit their access to resources because, if they do, a competitor can enter the market and beat them at their own game. However, market control only works when organizations produce products or services that can be unambiguously defined and priced, and when competition makes prices meaningful. As transaction cost economist Oliver Williamson (1932– ) showed, absent these conditions markets become inefficient and ultimately fail.

59

An alternative to using competition to discipline organizational behavior involves rules and regulations written and upheld by those possessing hierarchical authority. But hierarchy and the bureaucracy it creates come with their own well-known failures. In a stable and unchanging world, bureaucratic organizations work well enough, but in times of rapid change they have trouble keeping current with evolving needs. Their resistance to change combined with rule-mindedness render bureaucracies self-focused and maladaptive, hence unresponsive to environmental pressures.

When markets cannot set prices efficiently, and bureaucracies cannot respond fast enough to keep up with environmental change, neither markets nor bureaucracies provide adequate control to protect society from an imbalance of power in favor of those who control organizations. How then can the institutional order control the organizations meant to serve it, particularly when global organizations outgrow their host communities and nations? One possibility is through organized social action typically seen in social movements such as those urging ethical governance, ecological sustainability, and social equity.

Social movements represent emerging efforts to (re)gain control over massive corporations and national governments. These become particularly interesting when the movements go global, giving them the same power and reach the largest corporations and governments enjoy. It remains to be seen if new organizations produced by these movements, such as non-governmental organizations (NGOs), can influence the institutional order enough to redress the balance of power between business and society.

The Red Cross achieved institutional status many years ago and offers a model many NGOs follow. Its legitimacy gives it global influence over government agencies and corporate actors and permits it to attract funding for some projects from these sources. Will the intertwining interests of institutions like the Red Cross form a new institutional order able to control the exploitation of our planet's resources? Or will it simply contribute another layer of complexity rendering control more difficult than ever?

Even if social movements succeed in controlling or at least influencing global corporations and governments to change their worst behaviors, we will no doubt continue to depend upon corporations and governments, hoping that, when it proves necessary, we can change our institutions in time to prevent disaster. There is reason to believe this is possible because, in spite of the stabilizing role they play in society, institutions do sometimes change.

The institution of marriage has come under tremendous pressure in the US in recent years by those who believe that everyone has the right to marry and raise a family, including homosexuals. For US citizens, pressures to change the institutional rules of marriage raise fundamental questions about how marriage should be defined. Is it a license granted (i.e. by church or state), or a contract like any other in which citizens have a right to freely enter? If it is the latter, then the power of the church to decide who participates and how they do so may be significantly reduced, limiting the scope of that institution and transferring some of its power and influence to other institutions, for example courts of law.

This potential redrawing of the boundaries that define institutional territory has not surprisingly triggered resistance from US churches as well as debates about other social issues, such as the freedom of women to divorce their husbands, cohabitation outside marriage, and the practices of contraception and abortion. Such embeddedness in the larger institutional order helps to explain why it is difficult for the institution of marriage to change. Even so, institutions *will* change as mindsets alter with time and experience. It is a question of what people get used to. Now that the right to be openly gay in the military has passed into law, can gay marriage be far behind?

As you can see, there is good news and bad news. While institutions limit confusion and make social life stable and predictable, they also limit creativity, innovation, and, consequently, change. This is because their reliance on mindless reproduction of the social order makes it hard for new meaning to occur. Because culture theory treats meaning more dynamically, it offers a better framework for understanding change than does institutional theory, but be sure to notice the close relationship between culture and institutions. In my view, culture thrives where conscious thought and feeling inform action, whereas institutions move out of this territory into realms of mindlessness. In that sense, today's institutions are the slowly decaying remains of yesterday's culture.

## Organizational culture and symbolism

In any social group, including organizations, members develop a system of intersecting meanings to orient themselves to one another and coordinate their activities. This socially constructed meaning system emerges from the interpretations people give to their life together. It influences behavior and gives things (objects, events, words) their symbolic significance.

In a way, culture is a repository for the symbols and artifacts that its members produce, but it is also the product of their collective sensemaking and, at the same time, the context within which meaning is continuously made and remade. All this is what cultural anthropologist Clifford Geertz meant when he said: 'man is an animal suspended in webs of significance he himself has spun.' Geertz's definition of culture as those webs of significance helped turn the attention of organizational culture researchers to symbols and symbolic action.

Relying on cultural anthropologists whose work also influenced Geertz, social psychologist Edgar Schein (1928– ) gave culture a more functional definition: 'The pattern of basic assumptions that a given group has invented, discovered, or developed in learning to cope with its problems of external adaptation and internal integration, and that have worked well enough to be considered valid, and, therefore, to be taught to new members as the correct way to perceive, think, and feel in relation to these problems.' Be sure to notice how external adaptation indicates that organizational culture is related to the environment, while internal integration relates culture to the organization's social and physical structures and technology.

In spite of the widespread influence of Schein's definition, most research on organizational culture emphasizes internal integration, giving limited attention to culture as a mechanism by which organizations adapt to their environments. Managers, too, overemphasize internal integration when they accuse organizational cultures of creating resistance to change without sufficiently appreciating the many ways that culture leads to and supports change. Pasquale Gagliardi split the difference, observing paradoxically that, 'organizations change in order to remain the same.' The thing to remember is that organizational culture simultaneously enables both stability *and* change.

According to Schein, organizational culture lies in the depths of collective meaning that express basic assumptions about life, such as our relationship to time (are we focused more on the past, present, or future?), nature (are we master, co-worker, or pawn?), and other human beings (are we hierarchical, democratic, individualistic, collectivist?). These assumptions manifest as the values that guide our behavior. Culturally influenced behavior, in turn, produces artifacts that realize (make real) cultural values and the assumptions that underpin them.

Knowing what artifacts mean and how to behave in an acceptable manner is a sign of cultural membership. From how to dress for work to what to say to the big boss, solutions to mundane problems and sacred taboos are communicated through meaning-laden

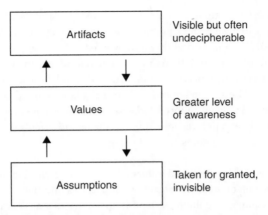

| Artifacts | Visible but often undecipherable |
| Values | Greater level of awareness |
| Assumptions | Taken for granted, invisible |

**13. Schein's model of organizational culture as assumptions, values, and artifacts**

artifacts known as symbols. Symbols and symbolism lead us to an appreciation of how cultures are socially constructed via sensemaking and how this affects organizations.

## Symbols and the complexity of accounting for cultural meaning

Not every artifact is a symbol, though any artifact could be. A cultural symbol is created whenever cultural members associate particular meanings with an artifact. Therefore a symbol is something that stands for something else, as when citizens of a country associate feelings of nationalism with their flag. Experiencing national pride in a flag's presence renews the artifact's symbolism, as do any other communicative purposes to which the flag is put (e.g. saluting, waving, burning).

Some artifacts come to always signify a particular meaning. In the context of war, a white flag signals surrender. Culture meets institution in this example because the white flag as a cultural symbol has become an institution within the international institutional order of warfare. In this context, the flag's meaning is

| Category | Examples |
|---|---|
| Objects | Art/design/logo |
| | Architecture/décor/furnishings |
| | Dress/appearance/costume/uniform |
| | Products/equipment/tools |
| | Displays of posters/photos/memorabilia/cartoons |
| | Signage |
| Verbal expressions | Jargon/names/nicknames |
| | Explanations/theories |
| | Stories/myths/legends and their heroes and villains |
| | Superstitions/rumors |
| | Humor/jokes |
| | Metaphors/proverbs/slogans |
| | Speeches/rhetoric/oratory |
| Activities | Ceremonies/rituals/rites of passage |
| | Meetings/retreats/parties |
| | Communication patterns |
| | Traditions/customs/social routines |
| | Gestures |
| | Play/recreation/games |
| | Rewards/punishments |

14. **Artifacts can take many forms, but all are objects, words, or deeds, or some combination of these**

fixed and unquestioned (institutionalized) and communicates across cultures.

In contrast to the meaning of signs, symbolic meaning remains interpretively open, allowing some symbols to carry multiple and often conflicted messages and to be used for competing purposes. For example, some people burn flags or holy books that are sacred to others. These examples show that symbolic meaning is constructed around and through artifacts people use as they interact and communicate to themselves and with others.

While symbols are often shared, their interpretations may and usually do differ, particularly as time passes. Consider all the different ideas represented by the swastika over the centuries. The swastika first appeared in Neolithic times and has been used continuously up to the present day, for example, with religious significance given to it by Buddhists, Hindus, and Jains. Meanwhile, for Holocaust victims and those who sympathize with them, the swastika's original Sanskrit meaning of wellbeing was perverted by association with Nazism, while neo-Nazis continue to interpret it as a symbol of their ideology.

The occurrence of multiple meanings for cultural symbols is part of what makes culture so rich and also so difficult to control. For those who produce an artifact with a symbolic purpose in mind, meaning may be clear-cut and direct, but once others adopt the artifact as their symbol, they will use it to express their own meanings. For example, fans use corporate logos and slogans to express their affinity with a brand or company, while critics use the same symbols to embarrass the organization, such as when the McDonald's logo is attached to pictures of obese children, or the slogan 'Marlboro Country' adorns the image of a cemetery.

Symbols are constantly being created and changed through expression as novel meaning is produced or old meaning takes new forms. This suggests that, not only do symbolic meanings multiply, multiple meanings will constantly shift about. Shifting meaning indicates that the processes of meaning-making are active and engaging.

Active engagement with cultural processes, in my view, is what produces the perception that culture is shared. The sharing of culture through sensemaking, rather than the making of particular meanings, could account for why no one has ever specified what is the shared meaning of a culture to the satisfaction of all its members. What we share is artifacts and our experiences of making meaning together with them, but not necessarily our interpretations of what a particular symbol means. Even though we cannot agree on their meanings, still we share our culture by celebrating certain artifacts and making them our symbols. In this way, we do not have to agree on the substance of symbolic meaning, and may not even want to. After all, our differences contribute to the ability of culture to adapt to new situations just as our similarities provide a sense of comfort and stability.

## Socialization and the element of surprise

Symbols will usually only be recognized by those initiated into the ways of the culture, which makes entering a new culture tricky. Though the symbolic material of culture is publicly available to everyone, only members of the culture will recognize and understand the meanings their symbols carry. Acquiring cultural knowledge, therefore, demands a period of socialization for children born into the culture, or of acculturation for outsiders who wish to join. During socialization, cultural insiders use a range of sanctions, from teasing to physical punishment, to orient the newcomer to culturally appropriate ways of thinking, behaving, and communicating with symbols.

However, since the bulk of cultural knowledge is tacit, it cannot be communicated directly. In fact, direct communication may be counterproductive to learning a culture both because a culture's members know much more than they can say, and because they sometimes say one thing and do another. Following stated rules or advice is not likely to translate fully the complex meaning system that is culture. The tacit norms, values, and assumptions that inform meaning-making are most often transferred to new members through the many experiences and contexts of daily life that embed them in the culture.

But even fully socialized members of a culture can be surprised by the interpretive turns symbolic meaning can take. In the town where I grew up, Notre Dame University constructed a new campus library. Decision-makers deliberately designed and situated the building centrally on campus with the intention to

**15. Potent symbolism adorns the main library on the campus of Notre Dame University in South Bend, Indiana**

symbolize the religious heritage of this Roman Catholic institution. The building wore a mosaic featuring the figure of Christ, arms outstretched and raised toward heaven.

Most members of Notre Dame University celebrate the many championship football teams the school has contributed to college athletics over the years. In American football, when one team scores a goal, the official in charge indicates the 'touchdown' by raising his outstretched arms in a gesture similar to the one depicted by the mosaic. Although the library was located quite close to the football stadium, apparently none of the decision-makers anticipated the connection students would make between the two key symbols of campus culture – football and Christ. Upon its unveiling, students christened the library's mosaic 'Touchdown Jesus.'

'Touchdown Jesus' makes an important point about organizational culture: You cannot always anticipate, and certainly cannot control, the meanings members of a culture give to the symbols they socially construct through their sensemaking. The authorities of Notre Dame University probably would have preferred a different tagline for the mosaic, but they got the one the culture produced. There is only so much cultural engineering possible, which is why culture offers a different metaphor than that of the machine.

In relation to the metaphors for organizations, be sure to notice how the idea of engineering a culture, so attractive to managers hoping to control others via cultural values, norms, and expectations, befits the metaphor of the psychic prison more than that of culture itself. The psychic prison metaphor brings with it the question of power and suggests looking into the matter of relationships between organizational subcultures.

## Subcultures

In a social group that grows beyond small numbers, the possibility of culture dividing into subcultures arises. Division of labor, physical separation of different activities, delegated authority, and internal competition for power and status all serve to create differentiation within an organization. As members of a group interact repeatedly, they develop their own ways of working together and jargon and other symbols for expressing their meaning to one another. These create the conditions for subcultures to emerge. One subculture that is particularly pronounced in many organizations is the subculture populated by top management.

The top management subculture produces corporate culture, that is the culture desired and formally communicated by top management. Take care not to confuse corporate with organizational culture. The organizational culture is socially constructed by the entire organization. This includes top managers, but because sensemaking is distributed throughout the organization, top managers can never fully control it. Top management's influence comes not only through communicating the corporate culture, but also via top management's own behavior. Their influence, regardless of its source, is moderated by power relationships between organizational subcultures, and distributed throughout the organization.

Due to the relative power of hierarchical authority, non-dominant subcultures usually orient themselves around the top management subculture. Most will publicly embrace the corporate culture in order to maintain themselves as members in good standing. However, this does not always mean their subculture is in harmony with or even supportive of the corporate culture. A counter-cultural orientation to top management will sometimes occur in organizations, just as it does in societies. Thus power relationships can create different subcultures within organizations.

Other differences that can create subcultures in organizations may result from occupations (e.g. doctors, nurses, anesthesiologists, social workers, and administrators in a hospital); functional specialties (e.g. marketing, finance, human resources); geographic locations (e.g. east, west, north, south); tenure (e.g. old guard, new kids); or identity (e.g. gender, race, ethnicity, or sexual orientation). A given organizational subculture may be a mixture of any of these differentiating factors including power relationships, and members of a culture can easily belong to more than one subculture. Individuals can also switch their affiliations over time, as happens, for example, when an employee is promoted to the rank of manager.

Subcultures are one way to think about divisions of difference within organizations. Departmentalization, part of social structure, is another. No matter what internal divisions appear, power will not be far away.

# Chapter 4
# **Who does organizing serve?**

Any living creature gets embroiled in power struggles when needed or desired resources are limited. These conditions define competition and the exercise of relative power determines who wins. Competition affects organizations both externally and internally. Externally, organizations compete to control the resources that ensure their survival, while internally, individuals compete for top jobs, lucrative wages, and the status and power that these provide. Competition to determine control over power sources leads to political behavior.

Power and politics captivate the attention of those critical of capitalism and the management practices that support it. They often refer to Karl Marx's theory of the effects of domination on relationships between social classes. Marx asked questions like: Why do dominated groups consent to their own exploitation? And why do they sometimes even conspire with those who dominate them? He believed that social, economic, and political structures underpin power relationships, which in turn are based on domination.

According to Marx's many followers, one way to define capitalist organizations is as the economic expression of the desire to dominate others. This motivation explains the politics of organizational decision-making processes as well as the politics of identity, a term used to describe the struggle to embrace diversity resulting from differences in gender, race, ethnicity, and sexual orientation. The politics of identity reveals one of domination's ugliest effects – oppression.

Inspired by Marx, capitalism's critics believe that the benefits of autonomy (e.g. personal freedom, human development, creativity) are unnecessarily constrained and distorted by capitalism and the practice of management. They offer communication and decision-making processes that involve a full range of stakeholder interests as antidotes to the negative effects of domination in the belief that, when whole persons are fully engaged, values for family, health, and human decency will win out over those serving only moneyed interests. Workplace democracy and corporate citizenship exemplify the organization of stakeholder influence intended to reduce the negative effects of domination within corporations.

But not everyone concerned with organizational power and politics takes a critical view. There are those who simply want to acknowledge and understand the role power plays in organizations, while others want this knowledge so they can use organizational politics to their own advantage. Whatever your reasons, it is a safe bet that any organization with which you come into contact will be shaped, at least to some extent, by these forces.

## Power, politics, and dependence

A widely used definition of power is one's capacity to influence someone else. Individuals confront many sources of power in organizations, all of which are built into interpersonal relationships. This is what it means to say that power is relational. For example, formal authority derives from one's position and thus from relationships between those at the top and bottom of an organizational hierarchy. But there are many other sources of power than those defined by hierarchical relationships.

A personality or physical appearance attractive to others produces personal power. The possession of skills, knowledge, or information that others need provides expertise power. The power of coercion derives from a threat of force strong enough to compel others to take actions they otherwise would not take, or to espouse attitudes they do not really hold. Control of scarce and/or critical material resources such as budgets, raw materials, equipment, the supply of labor, and physical space produces resource-based power over those who desire or need these resources. Controlling the access others have to powerful persons or information gives opportunistic power to those who control access.

Power relationships are often complex. For example, even those with the most formal authority (e.g. a king or queen, the president of a nation, a CEO) depend on the expertise of their advisors who, in turn, use their access to the powerful to gain advantages over others. And while authority may seem to grant total control to those at the top of a hierarchy, it must be weighed against the power lower-level participants hold. For example, workers who maintain the equipment that drives production can use their knowledge to counteract the power of those in charge.

When a machine breaks, managers who depend on production to meet goals and earn their bonuses become dependent on anyone who can repair it. That machines break down gives maintenance workers considerable power so long as they maintain their control over the knowledge required to fix the machine. The struggle for control over sources of power that can counteract that of management produced the institutions of the labor contract and the labor union.

There are important differences between formal authority and other sources of power, sometimes called informal powers to distinguish them from formal authority. One of them is that the exercise of formal authority is directed downward in organizations, while the exercise of power rooted in other sources is typically directed upward or laterally, either across individuals or across organizational units. A workers' strike against management is an example of applying power upwards, while hoarding information critical to a colleague is a lateral power play that occurs in the relationship between certain individuals. Turf wars between functions or other organizational departments exemplify lateral power plays that take place between different groups.

Using formal authority has fewer costs than does using informal power. Exercising informal power usually requires an expenditure of resources such as knowledge or personal attention, or making commitments or concessions regarding one decision in exchange for support on another. Once expended, informal power is depleted and power holders must renew it or suffer the erosion of their influence. For example, a person with control over the assignment of office spaces gleans power from the control of this resource only until they make the assignments. A person who overuses their personal attractiveness comes to be seen as manipulative with a consequent loss of personal power.

By comparison, the exercise of formal authority is not diminished by use and can even be enhanced by it. Power that is institutionalized in formal authority creates expectations such that *not* exercising formal power may provoke questions about the powerholder's hold on his or her power. 'Use it or lose it' applies particularly well here.

The pressure to use formal authority and the motivation to offset it by using power that is then in need of replenishment keeps an organization's power distribution in constant flux. Recurring efforts to find the balance point of power when circumstances change or new issues arise produce organizational politics.

Many people consider politics to be inappropriate in organizations because political processes undermine rationality, thereby creating suboptimal decisions. Nevertheless, spending time in pretty much any organization will reveal undeniable evidence of political behavior. One of the naïve mistakes rookie managers make is to present a 'rock solid' (i.e. irrefutably rational) case for a decision, only to have it denied by those who later will advise the newcomer how to work the system to achieve a better outcome in the future. Political scientist Herbert Simon (1916–2001) explained this phenomenon with his theory of bounded rationality, which was in part responsible for his Nobel Prize in Economics, awarded in 1978.

According to Simon, decision-making is only rational under highly restrictive conditions that rarely occur in organizations, namely that known problems have unambiguous solutions. When these conditions do not hold, bounded rationality prevails. This is a phenomenon in which, while still holding rationality as an ideal, decision-makers 'satisfice' (a blend of the words satisfy and suffice) by seeking a solution that is adequate rather than optimal.

Has your family ever decided to go somewhere or do something simply because it was a choice everybody could agree upon, perhaps going to see a movie nobody really wanted to see? If so, you have satisficed. In a way, satisficing involves optimization, but it is optimization that takes the costs of coming to agreement into account. When a decision falls short of the stated goal or intention of decision-makers because they find that it takes too much time, effort, or money to find the 'best' solution, then they are satisficing in the same manner that took your family to that movie nobody wanted to see.

Conflicting interests, competition over scarce resources, and complex interdependence among actors and problems all violate the conditions for rationality in decision-making processes and all are common within organizations. Under these conditions, the definition of what is optimal becomes contentious, and the contention can usually only be resolved through a political process such as working the system before a decision is formally made.

Bounded rationality politicizes decision-making processes when less influential decision-makers align their interests behind a jointly favored alternative in order to offset the influence of more powerful decision-makers, who, in turn, are forced to align themselves to retain their political dominance. The realignment continues until the decision can be made. This is known as coalition-building, and its result is the support of a decision favoring one set of aligned internal interests over others.

Because new problems constantly arise, political maneuvering in organizations is endless. When coalition-building becomes an everyday occurrence, it is hard not to see organizations primarily as arenas for power and politics where everyone constantly barters their support to get decisions made.

But the sources of organizational power lie not just within organizations, they extend into the environment and boomerang back again. The environment uses its power to demand competitive prices, desirable products and services, and efficient organizational structures and processes. This is done institutionally, for example through legislation and regulation, but also through the power dynamics embedded in relationships between the organization and its many stakeholders.

The environment has power over organizations because organizations need resources that other organizational actors within the environment control. A complex set of dependencies exists between the organization and those who provide its resources (Figure 16). Suppliers sell the organization their raw materials and equipment, while customers consume its products and services,

Knowledge
(technological
sector)

Labor
(economic,
social, and
cultural sectors)

Raw Material
(physical
sector)

Organization

Revenue
(economic
sector)

Capital
(economic
sector)

Legitimacy
(social, cultural,
legal, political
sectors)

16. **Organizations depend on their environments for capital, raw materials, knowledge, labor, revenue, and legitimacy (sectors from which these resources are drawn shown in parentheses)**

Who does organizing serve?

investors and lenders supply capital, employment agencies provide labor, and universities and think tanks offer knowledge.

Competitors, regulatory agencies, and special interest groups can also affect an organization's chances for survival and success. Competitors affect the availability and prices of raw material and labor, and compete for customers and the best employees. Regulatory agencies such as tax authorities, licensing agents, and customs inspectors affect profits and can impede business transactions. Special interests – groups that want to influence various organizational activities – can apply a mix of political, economic, social, and cultural pressures to influence organizational decision-making and behavior.

NGOs, for example, may demand that an organization address issues ranging from world health, human rights, and fair trade, to shareholder rights, family and work-life balance, inequalities of identity groups such as those based on gender or race, and environmental and consumer protection. Of course, organizations have their own special interest groups. Trade associations hire lobbyists to pressure government officials and legislators on behalf of the businesses they represent.

Organizations specialize functionally or divisionally, in part to help them manage their external dependencies, and this creates another source of power inside organizations. As organization theorists Jeffrey Pfeffer (1946– ) and Gerald Salancik (1943–96) pointed out, any group that can manage a critical dependence on the environment on behalf of the organization gains power within it.

Marketing, for example, manages market dependencies by stimulating sales, serving existing customers, and locating and attracting new ones. Corporate communication counteracts negative public opinion and the influence of special interest groups with corporate image campaigns and corporate citizenship programs. Human resources (HR) manages labor and knowledge dependencies with strategies for recruiting needed personnel and retaining them. Finance manages cash flow and can generate a revenue stream independent of selling products and services by leveraging assets such as investing unused cash.

Internally, the relative power of organizational units is determined by the effectiveness with which they manage critical external dependencies on behalf of the organization. This means that external influence works its way into the power bases of units and positions inside the organization. Furthermore, when individuals or units use this power to promote their own interests (e.g. to influence the outcome of budget requests), organizational structure is shaped by the organization's external relationships.

This internal power-alignment process is one way in which organizations come to look like their environments. It explains why power and politics are central to understanding organizations. In this explanation, power and politics still derive from domination, but their dynamics occur between organizations operating in an environment as well as among individuals working within the organization.

Power dynamics thus thoroughly permeate organizations and thereby subject them to the effects of domination, as argued by Marx. But power can be more than domination, as was pointed out by sociologist Mary Parker Follett (1868–1933), a prominent 20th-century proponent of democracy. In opposition to Marx, Follett proposed the idea that power is a source of creative energy. She saw the process of creating joint power over a conflict situation as an alternative to viewing power as a competitive force based in domination.

Follett considered domination to be only one of three possible approaches to conflict resolution. She saw compromise, the second strategy, as similarly negative in that none of the parties' interests are served completely. Of the three, only integration respects everyone's interests by realizing them all in a creative redefinition of the problem.

Follett illustrated integration using the example of two people reading in a library. One wants to open a window while the other prefers to keep it shut. While one person might dominate and thereby exercise their will at the expense of the other's interests, Follett suggested opening a window in an adjoining room. She arrived at this integrative solution by recognizing that the person who wants the window open really only desires fresh air, while the person who wants it closed merely does not want the wind to blow directly on them. Finding an alternative to opening the window is no compromise, according to Follett, because both parties get what they want: fresh air, no wind.

Follett's ideas about power have yet to have much impact on organizations and their managers who remain focused, for the most part, on domination and compromise. Some feminists attribute the slow uptake of Follett's ideas to her gender and point to her limited influence as being one consequence of the politics of identity, which is another way to think about what power in organizations means and how it works.

## The politics of identity and diversity

Feminists often argue that stereotypes cause us to discredit and devalue some members of society. They point to the fact that the high-paying, prestigious jobs that carry with them the greatest social status and power are inequitably distributed across many dimensions of social identity, including gender, race, ethnicity, religious or sexual preference, and age. Stereotypes of marginalized identity groups serve to make it seem natural that their members take certain jobs or occupy particular roles, typically those offering lower pay and conferring less power and status. The disproportion of white males in positions of power and authority across capitalistic societies provides convincing evidence.

A popular idea among feminists is that work in private life is associated with the feminine ideals of caring and community, while work in public life is rational and competitive, characteristics long associated with the stereotypical male. A number of feminist scholars have argued that this public/private separation of male and female domains reinforces a dualistic view of gender that helps to define the identities of men and women and shapes interaction between them.

Dualism refers to the relationship between two opposing terms, which can be seen as complementary ('you are the yin to my yang') or contradictory ('are you for or against me?'). Feminists argue that dualism reinforces traditional relations of domination/subordination, thus perpetuating the existing social order. In addition to public/private, other dualisms – rational/emotional, hard/soft, active/passive – similarly underscore male/female differences, allowing them to endure in the face of persistent calls to redefine gender relations.

To see how pervasive this effect can be, try reading each of the pairs mentioned above in reverse order (e.g. emotional/rational). Does it feel strange to do this? Feminists often substitute 'she' for 'he' in their writing to normalize the feminine in language and make focusing on women as familiar as is the focus upon men. To the extent that the exercise above did not make you uncomfortable, perhaps they have succeeded!

Feminist sociologist Joan Acker (1924– ) transferred ideas about gender to organizations when she introduced the concept of gendered organizations. Assuming that gender is constructed by social practices that produce gender-based power relations, Acker argued that those in power determine important outcomes using language in gendered (i.e. non-gender-neutral) ways. When those in power are mostly male, they dominate the discourse that keeps them in power, including how women will be described and evaluated, and thus relegated to less influential jobs with lower status and power. Such attitudes socially construct organizations that are gendered through and through.

A consulting firm once asked me to observe and give feedback on their employee evaluation process. As each employee's name came up for consideration during the annual determination of raises and promotions, I noted the language used by those performing the evaluations, all of them men. Whereas the male candidates were never described by the word 'aggressive,' all the women were, and what is more, each woman was described as either too aggressive or not aggressive enough.

Not only was the aggression criterion never applied to the male candidates, it was used to justify lower raises and no promotions for any of the women. When I pointed this out, the evaluators expressed incredulity, but also some embarrassment. Such observations are not restricted to gender relations but extend to race, ethnicity, and other dimensions of diversity. For example, US President Barack Obama, whose mother was white and whose father was black, has been described as both 'too black' and 'not black enough.'

The gendering of organizations, or any other basis for stereotyping and discrimination, is not just a matter of words, it produces material reality. For example, sociologist and anthropologist Pierre Bourdieu (1930–2002) described how the Kabyle build relations between men and women into their houses. This African Berber tribe divide their residences into two sections separated by half a wall. One section is larger and higher than the other and paved with clay and cow dung polished to a high sheen by the women of the house. This larger space, regarded as 'male,' is used for eating and entertaining guests, in contrast to the smaller 'female' space, in which animals are kept beneath a loft where the women and children sleep and where tools and animal feed are stored. The Kabyle associate the male space with words like high, light, cooked, dry culture, whereas they associate female space with low, dark, raw, wet nature.

Human relationships become gendered in ways such as those demonstrated by Kabyle culture. That is, gender is symbolically and linguistically built into social life even as it is literally built into the physical world. The thousands of small symbols that collectively tell members who they are and how to behave create expectations and produce norms that give culture the power to define and maintain gender differences. Gender and other dimensions of human diversity form the cultural ground on which identity walks.

Power relationships create patterns of domination within organizations and these often favor one gender, race, ethnicity, age group, sexual orientation, and/or religious affiliation over others. This favoring is done at such a deep level that those who are dominant often do not recognize how they are privileged by the cultures their dominance has shaped. Of course, even those who dominate are not able to attain autonomy on their own terms or for long. This is as true for non-human social species as it is for humans.

If you drive one mile east on Route 133 in Ipswich, Massachusetts, where I live, you will find Wolf Hollow. There, a local family hosts a pack of wolves with the aid of a naturalist and some volunteers. If you stop to visit, you will learn that wolf packs are notoriously hierarchical and that a pack needs a leader to function. Typically, an alpha male plays this role, but a female can also lead. The Wolf Hollow pack suffered a setback some years ago when its lead wolf died, spurring the hosts to search for a suitable adolescent male. The replacement they located had a sister to whom he was deeply attached. They brought both to Wolf Hollow.

As the new wolves matured, the male was accepted by the pack and took on the role of alpha as expected. His sister Jelly was having more trouble fitting in. Always strong and aggressive enough to dominate her brother, Jelly began using her power over him in ways that subverted the pack's hierarchy. For example, at mealtime she would insist on being the first to eat and then lie down on the rest of the food so that the other wolves could not get to it. Her brother could not reprimand her because she could beat him in a fight (after one altercation, he had to have stitches!). The only remedy the hosts could find was to move Jelly to another enclosure.

In the wild, Jelly would probably have become what wolf experts call a disseminator, leaving one pack to start another. This would allow her to exercise her power without destroying the local social order. But because Jelly was raised in captivity, she could not survive in the wild, being overly trusting of humans. She was placed in a pen near to the pack, but she was no longer part of it. Though she howled and complained, for the sake of the pack she remained isolated. Life in the wolf pack went on like this until a sympathetic human volunteer asked to sit with Jelly to relieve her loneliness. Jelly came to accept the companionship of this kind soul, and today she greets her human companion with 15-foot leaps into the air and big wet kisses.

What can we say about Jelly and the disruption she caused, of the human responses to her situation, and, most importantly for our purposes, about the reorganization of the group of wolves that (re)established traditionally defined gender roles? One thing you might conclude is that wolf packs do not differ much from human organizations. The strongest males compete to determine who will lead, enjoying the perquisites of their status and accepting the responsibilities of leadership, such as defending the pack and keeping everyone in their place. The hierarchical order in the pack determines who will eat first and therefore how much, who must defer to whom, and even how high one can hold their tail. This was the order threatened by Jelly's behavior when she discovered her brother could not control her and tried to usurp his leadership position.

The solution to isolate Jelly will not be unfamiliar to those who, in human society, are sometimes referred to as strong women. Such women are unlikely to be accepted by their alpha male colleagues, and in organizations they are rarely welcomed by the 'pack' which includes other women (though less powerful females may encourage the competition between genders behind the scenes where the males won't see). When strong women take positions of authority, they meet the same challenges mounted toward their alpha male colleagues, with one big difference. Because they are female, a threatened male may not only believe he has a right to challenge her, but that she has no right to compete with men.

The isolation Jelly suffered is another aspect of power relations typical in hierarchically gendered societies. The best strategy to combat the need to deal with a strong female is to prevent her from taking a role in the 'pack' and, if feasible, not allow her to have any children. This can be symbolic, in the sense of not allowing her to have subordinates by blocking her promotion (e.g. on the grounds 'she is too aggressive'), or literal in the sense of being rejected by potential mates. If the strong woman does not submit to the expectation of being 'properly' female, she will be isolated in one or all of the available ways. Once isolated, it is nearly impossible for her to act as a role model for others, rendering her powerless in the eyes of others and, *de facto*, subordinated, even when she continues to behave in her dominant fashion toward men.

Now you may say that humans are not wolves and strong women do start their own companies and raise families. They sometimes even come to dominate organizations comprised mostly of men. Is this not proof that humans have more behavioral alternatives than wolves? Undoubtedly, but consider the possibility that the same unquestioned right of the host family to isolate Jelly and, using the logic that she would not be a fit mother, keep her from bearing offspring, is why even after many years of so-called feminine equality in many human societies, males still dominate most organizations. Similar stories can be told about those who are not white, not straight, not 'manly,' or not whatever defines the dominant group. Even after countless studies have shown the enormous benefits of diversity, you have to ask: Are we just wolves in human clothing?

Returning to Wolf Hollow, I continue to wonder whether, without human intervention, the pack would eventually have accepted Jelly as their leader. Was her food-hogging behavior just the first move in a change process only partly completed when the human caretakers imposed their gender stereotypes? After all, some wolf packs in the wild *are* led by alpha females.

# Critical postmodern voices

Feminists are not alone in finding fault with the consequences of human hierarchy and (ab)uses of organizational power. As already noted, Marx and his followers criticized capitalism and the effects of domination. These criticisms gained new adherents and energy from postmodernism, a late 20th-century philosophy that extended explanations of the role power plays in oppression, violence, and inequality. Noting power's propensity to hide in language and institutions, critical postmodernists offered new ways to think about ourselves in relation to organizations. According to them, it all started with the Enlightenment...

*El sueño de la razón produce monstruos* ('The Sleep of Reason Produces Monsters') is written on the side of the drawing table on which Francisco Goya (1746–1828) sleeps in a self-portrait by an artist many consider the last of the Old Masters. The air over the sleeping figure's head swarms with ominous bats and owls, symbols of disorder to educated 18th-century Europeans.

At the time of the Enlightenment, ideas like the one depicted in Goya's etching represented the spreading belief that reason alone – the gift of an enlightened mind – could awaken humankind from its nightmare of superstition. But for post-modern philosopher Jean-François Lyotard (1924–98), reason was the nightmare from which humankind needed to awaken. In the two centuries separating Goya and Lyotard, the reverence for reason that gave us modernism had given way to postmodern reflections on how the ideology of reason led us astray.

In *The Postmodern Condition: A Report on Knowledge*, Lyotard referred disdainfully to the Enlightenment as a failed project fueled by the progress myth, namely that science will save us from any problems we face and lead us to universal truth and justice. He described the perpetuation of the progress myth as a grand

17. Francisco Goya's 'The Sleep of Reason Produces Monsters' (1797–9), Number 43 of 80 etchings from the series *Los Caprichos*

narrative, the story of scientific achievement based in the application of reason and of authority legitimized by expertise. Lyotard's provocative ideas thrust postmodernism into the public limelight.

Attacking some of modernism's most cherished beliefs by referring to them as the Enlightenment project and the progress myth, Lyotard argued that our unexamined belief in reason and the expertise and progress it brings disguises the latest version of totalitarianism – the unlimited authority to impose one set of ideological beliefs on all members of a society. He described the masquerade perpetuated by institutions such as education, government, and business by showing how the expert knowledge from which they are created masks its own political motivations while legitimizing particular ways of thinking, talking, and acting.

Consider, for example, this scenario about power in organizations. Managers hire consultants to help their organization mimic the best practices of other organizations. They do this knowing that performance improvements, which the same consultants who deliver best practice will also measure for the company, will bring them career advancement and increased power. And admiring the consultant's recognized expertise also reassures the organization and its owners that the managers are doing the best job they can!

In return for all this, consultants are granted a share of the company's wealth, which is under management's control. The money consultants make demonstrates, or rather socially constructs, the value of their expertise to others (symbolized by the client list). At the same time, their expertise validates, just as their consulting perpetuates, management as a profession requiring expertise. A nice system of mutual reinforcement, all of which rests on belief in the power of reason. The ideology of reason in this instance supports the belief that consultants espousing the methods of science can deliver best practice.

Unmasking such effects of the Enlightenment project supports the view that so-called facts and the knowledge they uphold are simply agreements to regard certain claims as true. Instead of Truth (the capital T indicates the idea that truth is sacrosanct), all we can know are claims made on its behalf – hence (small t) truth claims. Claims about truth are social constructions, and the powerful have the greatest influence when it comes to deciding what to regard as true.

An important implication of understanding truth as claims made about it is that knowledge does not endure. Sooner or later, every truth claim will be displaced. Postmodernists explain how this happens by referring to the dynamics of power. The distribution of expert power determines how a community defines knowledge, and since power distributions are dynamic, when the distribution changes, what is regarded to be truth changes with it.

Philosopher and historian Michel Foucault (1926–84) did his part to unmask the relationship between knowledge and power when he proclaimed that knowledge *is* power. Just as Einstein collapsed the notions of space and time into space-time, Foucault proposed the concept power-knowledge. By studying the history of psychiatric hospitals and prisons, he showed that psychiatrists and social workers used their expertise to establish categories like insanity and delinquency into which people were sorted for institutional treatment, often involving some form of incarceration.

Foucault claimed that by defining insanity and delinquency as problems society needed to address, psychiatrists and social workers established powerful social positions based in their self-proclaimed ability to protect society from those deemed dangerous or otherwise socially unsuitable. All of this came about, Foucault explained, by an insidious shifting of public discourse within which terms such as insanity and delinquency are defined and debated. The public always turns to experts for guidance on these matters. A recent debate concerning US history textbooks illustrates the role of public discourse and how it is shaped by the struggle to control knowledge.

Publishers in the US look to the Texas Board of Education, as do other states, for signals concerning what content textbooks should cover. Texas buys more textbooks than any other state (its source of power over the publishers) and has a more unified view of what should constitute US history than other large customers, like California. Religious conservatives in Texas recently used their political influence to urge the Texas Board of Education to add new US history topics to high school textbooks, in particular creationism as an alternative to evolution and the recently popularized idea that the US was founded as a Christian mission from God.

The debate surrounding the content of history textbooks took place within the ongoing discourse about public schools in the US. Thus Foucault would have branded the claim that Christianity is a founding principle of the US as a discursive and highly political move. The critical postmodernist would worry that, if claimed as true in US textbooks, the espoused Christian beliefs could become dominant among the citizenry educated by these books.

The power of the textbook is no doubt overstated by this example given the youthful tendency to question the ideologies of their elders, but you get the idea. All knowledge, whether conservative, liberal, or otherwise, is sustained, not by objective Truth, whatever that might be, but by social constructions perpetuated in discourse that is biased by the motivations of the powerful. Although knowledge is forever open to change, its changes are always politically inflected.

Once you accept the idea that power influences knowledge, you can easily understand Lyotard's concern about the uses of power to silence opposition. He regarded silencing opposition as key to totalitarianism, pointing out that this occurs insidiously when a community has no procedures for preserving differences. Interestingly, Lyotard argued that when non-mainstream views and ideas are silenced, there can be no new ways to think or act, therefore, 'giving voice to silence' preserves innovation even as it combats totalitarianism.

The belief that free speech repels totalitarianism is one reason why so many of capitalism's critics and some postmodernists support democracy. And democracy's reliance on free and open discourse is why they worry over private ownership of media outlets. Conversely, those who criticize postmodernists argue that, in forming a shared ambition to overturn totalitarian tendencies, postmodernists merely privilege their own ideology. If there can be no overthrowing of privilege itself, then power-knowledge will prevail, as Foucault assured us it would.

What grand narrative, then, does postmodernism promote? In the Wachowski brothers' film *The Matrix*, we see a world taken over by artificial intelligence, in which machines breed and keep humans in pods as a power source for the computer that controls them all. The humans think they are living normal lives, but instead a computer program, the Matrix, simulates the world of the late 20th century. A much different world lies beyond the simulation in the nuclear wasteland of 21st-century reality.

The film's central character, symbolically named Neo, takes a pill that allows him to awaken from simulated reality. In order to survive and rescue others from the treachery of the machines that imprison them even as they tend to their every need, Neo has to move between post-nuclear reality where he and a small band of awakened humans battle the machines, and the pre-nuclear simulation. Whenever he re-enters the Matrix, Neo uses his knowledge that this reality is simulated to fight computer-generated superhuman bureaucrats. Denying simulated reality gives Neo the freedom and strength to thwart the villains and overthrow the machines. Ultimately, he prevails by challenging the computer program (and its invisible programmer), thereby crashing the Matrix.

*The Matrix* presents an allegory for critical postmodernism. In the same way that Neo escaped the Matrix in order to confront the computer program dominating all humankind, critical postmodernists want us to awaken from our Enlightenment-induced fantasies about the wonderful future reason will provide and face the difficult problems we have created for ourselves. Just as Neo's consciousness evolved as he confronted his fate, so must ours if we are to survive. Postmodernists do not claim to know the way exactly, they just provide an escape hatch to take us beyond the ideologies of the past. If this produces chaos, so be it.

# Chapter 5
# **How does organizing happen?**

The term 'organization' is most often opposed to chaos: organizations create order, whereas chaos brings disorder. The order organizing brought to humankind produced welcome stability and, thanks in large measure to the widely emulated examples of Rome's army and the Roman Catholic Church, bureaucracy became one of modern society's most prevalent features. While leadership was seen as essential to bringing order to these early times, its alter ego, management, as both a profession and an institution, evolved much later, tracing back to late 18th-century England and its industrializing textile factories, both products of the Enlightenment.

Factory managers then, as now, focused on delivering efficiencies brought about by the machine-driven standardization of work. They complemented this technology with the rules and routines of hierarchical bureaucracy, thereby more completely controlling workers. Standardization and mass production delivered the goods whose exchange built powerful economies. What is more, the repetition demanded by the machines allowed organizations to remain more or less the same over large stretches of time so that management practice could stabilize and develop into a recognized profession.

Longevity, stability, routines, and professionalism eventually turned industrial businesses into modern corporate institutions whose properties could be examined, understood, and designed to suit any purpose. During modernization, most of the change in the economic sector of industrialized nations came about by creating new organizations to serve slowly emerging needs and interests. The enormous size of many businesses gave these organizations disproportionate power that they used to buffer themselves from environmental pressures to change. Their bargain with society was that they would contribute social stability through millions of steady jobs in return for the economic growth brought by consumption of their goods and services. This worked because competition put downward pressure on prices, which continuously grew the economies of industrialized nations, made their citizens wealthy, and their corporations ever more powerful. But the power was increasingly concentrated in the hands of corporate owners and managers.

Eventually, the largest businesses outgrew their host nation's capacity to produce and consume, and they looked abroad for markets that could maintain or speed up their growth. At first, international companies such as IBM and Unilever concentrated on trade with other economically developed nations, but before long sought to develop productive capacity and markets in non-industrialized nations as well. In realizing their ambitions, they often benefited from government assistance in the forms of tax relief and sometimes direct funding.

Corporations soon realized they could develop local economies *and* enhance their profits by, for example, outsourcing labor intensive manufacturing activity to underdeveloped regions of the world where labor costs are low. Today the changes wrought by the activities of international corporations and their partners are weaving the economies of the world together by creating intricate networks of dependence out of capital flows. Globalization of economies, in turn, is altering cultures and societies all over the world.

One of the biggest changes organizations face is the rate of change in a globalizing world. No longer are managers trying to figure out how to standardize work; today, they spend most of their time trying to change it, or at least to keep up with its changes. Chronologically, the emphasis began shifting from stability to change around the end of World War II, when systems theory introduced the idea that organizations depend on their environments, and with uncertainty about the future brought by the war. There followed a period of steadily increasing change, or at least this is how most people experienced it.

It was during this period that managers began seeing adaptation as key to survival, and strategy as a mechanism to guide their organizations to success. Along with recognizing the importance of finding and maintaining an organization's strategic 'fit' within rapidly changing environments came the need to implement strategy through planned organizational change. Organizations and their products and services became tools to fight the chaos of uncertainty while managers battled the fear of change among employees.

As organizational change became focal for strategic management, particularly in globalizing firms such as Royal Dutch Shell, ABB, and GE, concerns about stability were delegated to technical specialists who worked in manufacturing (e.g. automobile assembly, the production of electronic goods, oil extraction and refining), or with improving service delivery (e.g. business consulting systems, fast food preparation, city management). As the managerial front line in the organizational war on chaos shifted from the shop floor to the executive suite, the field of organizational development (OD) grew up around the strategy movement and in support of the strategists.

In spite of all the change underway, early ideas about how organizing happens presented only static snapshots of organizations at successive points in time. This permitted comparisons *over* time but failed to address the third O – organiz*ing*, which happens *in* time. The idea of organizing as a dynamic process emerged from the shadows only when organizations started to be seen as ongoing accomplishments of sensemaking, social construction, and discourse.

Coming to terms with organiz*ing* requires process thinking, the roots of which reach back to ancient Greece where the philosopher Heraclitus (c. 535–475 BC) famously observed: 'You cannot step twice into the same river.' Ideas like those of process philosophy replace static notions of organization(s) with a vision of continually evolving processes. With this shift in thinking, the perpetual state of becoming that is organiz*ing* overtakes the static state of being that is organiz*ation(s)*. But let us begin where OD got its start, with the idea of developmental change.

## Organizational development and change

Like organisms, organizations develop over time. As is true for other living systems, their developmental progression is somewhat predictable. For example, organizations begin with a core activity around which, if they survive long enough, they will eventually build support, maintenance, and adaptive functions, typically in that order. Although, like humans, each organization finds its own way through the developmental stages of growth and decline, telling the story of one particular organization will give you the general idea of how developmental stages unfold.

In the late 1960s, three university students started making hand-tooled leather belts for themselves and their friends. Soon friends of friends were placing orders, and the entrepreneurs began earning enough money to cover extracurricular activities such as throwing parties. Not having to work for others had great appeal and, if they succeeded, they thought they could avoid taking corporate jobs after graduation.

One afternoon, the friends visited the local shopping mall and noticed a newly opened store catering to the latest fashion craze, blue jeans. They spoke to the store manager, who agreed to sell their belts, paying them only after sales were made. So, before they could produce their first order, they had to find money to invest in raw material. Up until then, they had spent all they had earned. One of the friends got a small loan from his parents, and they used the money to fill the living room in the house two of them shared with leather, dye, and belt buckles. They made belts in the kitchen.

Sales were brisk, but because it took time to collect their revenue, the friends always seemed to be out of cash. No more parties, but then they no longer had much time free anyway. They persevered, and eventually the revenue stream caught up and surpassed the cash needed to operate. But by this time, they had run out of space. They found it took as much time to switch operations between cutting, dying, and tooling the leather as it did to make the belts, and there was only room enough in the kitchen to do one operation at a time.

They moved to an old barn that gave them more room to work but increased their costs, requiring them to make and sell more belts just to break even. Fortunately, they could sell as many belts as they made. However, they desperately needed to increase their rate of production to cover expanding expenses.

Once they had more space, they found ways to organize that allowed them to work faster. For example, they saved considerable time by assigning the job of tooling to the person with the most artistic ability, thereby also reducing waste due to poor craftsmanship. The other two concentrated on cutting, punching, and dying leather. Once the leather was prepared, anyone could attach a buckle and add the finished belt to inventory. This meant adding it to a box under the finishing table. Whoever went out would deliver the box of inventory, take the next check to the bank, buy supplies, and bring back a couple of pizzas and some beer. The division of labor was emerging.

One evening after a long day's work, the friends relaxed with a beer behind the barn. Although he routinely skipped astronomy class, one of them could still point out Orion's Belt. The name stuck and not long after they started doing business as Orion's Belts, a regional chain of blue jean specialty shops opened locally and its manager noticed the many customers buying belts at his competitor's store. He contacted the company to see if they could supply his store as well and offered a contract that would double their sales revenue, and a check to cover the first order.

They signed the contract and ramped up for the new level of production by persuading some friends to help them make belts. This worked out well, with everyone coming to work when they felt like it and earning money according to the hours they put in. There was enough work to go around, but not so much that they had trouble keeping a little ahead of their orders. A comfortable inventory, and enough income to keep them in leather and buckles as well as spending money, kept everyone cool. The group helped themselves stay merry by having a keg of beer constantly on tap and taking spontaneous holidays to enjoy the weather together when it was particularly nice outside. The three friends had created the business of their hippie dreams.

Sales were so strong that other stores within the regional chain soon placed orders. In addition to making sales calls on existing customers, one of the founders began calling on other stores across the region. During these excursions, he often did market research by chatting with consumers to find out what sort of belts they liked and what else they might want, bringing ideas for new belt designs and other products like wallets and bags back to the company. As long as he was out driving around anyway, it made sense for him to purchase supplies, including beer and occasionally pizzas, before returning to the barn. It would not be long before purchasing and sales activities consumed nearly all his available time.

At this point, orders escalated dramatically, which meant more cash outlays and some stress on the two belt-making owners, who up until then had picked up any slack in production by skipping classes. Grades were falling. They realized they needed to hire more people. They hired friends of their friends and a few students they met in a local bar who seemed eager to earn a little extra cash. To make sure they covered their orders, they asked workers to sign up in advance for whatever number of hours per week they wanted, and for the most part their employees honored their commitments.

The company was still managing to cover production demands week by week, but the owners always felt stretched to the limit because someone would get sick, produce less than expected, or deliver poor quality. Recurring quality and scheduling issues convinced the two beltmakers that one of them should take formal responsibility for supervising the employees. This was tricky, since whoever took on this responsibility would have to drop out of school in order to be present during all working hours. To compensate him, an annual salary was set, and on the advice of one of their fathers, the three friends found a lawyer who wrote a partnership agreement for them.

By now, the requirements of using their technology, combined with environmental opportunities in the form of customer demand for their hand-tooled leather products, had shaped the structure of Orion's Belts from both inside and out. What was once an undifferentiated group of three people making belts around a kitchen table had become a technical core of workers specialized into cutting, tooling, punching, dyeing, and buckle-attaching tasks (Figure 18.1). This core was supported by a purchasing and sales function that brought in raw material, made sales, and distributed product to customers (Figure 18.2).

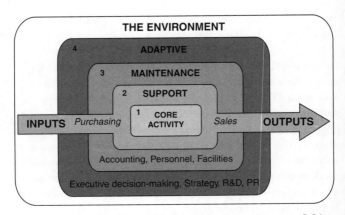

**18. Daniel Katz (1903–98) and Robert Kahn (1918– ) proposed this model of an organization's developmental stages: 1) A core activity focused on product or service delivery develops first, followed by 2) support, 3) maintenance, and 4) adaptive functions**

The manager's job was created to help the company integrate its newly differentiated functions via their supervision, but this move created more differentiation. The manager's job quickly grew to include the maintenance functions of keeping records, writing paychecks, paying suppliers, collecting sales revenue, and paying taxes. There were odd jobs to manage as well, such as fixing the leaky roof of the barn and filling holes in the driveway.

Before long, the supervising manager found it difficult to keep up with the payroll and tax issues, and collecting revenue from a customer base that kept growing was critical for managing the company's cash flow. He hired an accountant to free up some of his time to develop the business in new directions (Figure 18.3). Customers were clamoring for other hand-tooled leather products, and the idea of making wallets and tote bags had captured his imagination. He wanted to devote time to creating new product lines, the first sign that strategy was emerging (Figure 18.4). But before he could make any strategic moves, a major national retail chain called.

The partners agreed to produce belts for the national chain, but not before taking a hard look at their finances and their organization. They needed raw material, of course, but also insurance, more tools, including some machines for cutting leather, and a larger and more secure production facility. They also agreed to complement their new accountant with a personnel manager to recruit, train, and administer to the new employees they would need. They promoted the supervising partner to the role of managing director to oversee all this activity, and one of their senior employees took over the job as employee supervisor. A bank loaned them money, but insisted they set up an advisory board to help direct the firm's activities. Ironically, Orion's Belts was turning into the kind of corporate enterprise the founders had hoped never to work for!

Somehow they kept the business going and the managing director eventually relaxed some of the rules and regulations the advisory board had implemented. They reinstituted spontaneous holidays, and although nobody could drink alcohol at work any longer, they found ways to play that did not threaten anyone's life or limb. It was a happy enterprise, by and large, and a successful one until the bottom fell out of their market in the mid-1970s.

Orion's Belts suffered as hand-tooled leather goods lost popularity. As sales fell, they kept cutting back until there was nothing much left. In spite of the managing director's good intentions to do so, they let new opportunities to pursue the old business get in the way of their development. They had failed to fully develop the adaptive function (Figure 18.4) that might have allowed them to anticipate the market shift and reposition the business in time to save the company. Never mind, it was time for the friends to take those corporate jobs. And, with their background running their own business, they easily found lucrative positions.

The story of Orion's Belts shows how, as an organization matures, its technology and environment conspire to shape its structure, just as contingency theory suggests. But it also gives you a feeling for the human aspects of organizing. For example, you should notice that Orion's Belts was not only a business. The activities in which the founders and their employees engaged spawned a culture colored by their friendship and values about working in particular ways. This culture implicated the meaning of working together in acts of organizing that influenced how others would relate to the company, thus connecting the organization to its environment and shaping its identity at every stage of its development.

# The dynamics of organizational culture and identity

Whenever and wherever people interact, they produce culture and group identity. This happens as a consequence of human sensemaking and through social construction processes that transform artifacts into symbols, like the swimming parties Orion's Belts turned into a corporate rite of spring. Such symbols forge a sense of belonging to something larger than oneself.

## Culture and organizing

According to pragmatist philosopher John Dewey (1859–1952), physical reality becomes what it is as people find out what they mean by their creations. These meanings can then be communicated through symbols and thus will be elaborated by others, including their future selves. Symbols allow people to elaborate cultural meaning, as happens, for example, when telling stories about corporate swimming parties makes employees laugh in remembering a shared past that cements their future relationship with the company.

Over time, the accumulation of effects from symbolic activity surrounding emotion and meaning-laden artifacts produces the rich and varied web of significance that Geertz identified as culture. Culture thus connects people to each other by weaving together their identities, experiences, and memories. It also infuses their artifacts, the material part of culture, with their socially constructed meaning, as Dewey explained.

According to Dewey, 'inner' experiences captured in images, observations, memories, and emotions interpenetrate the physical material of artifacts to create cultural symbols. For example, even where nature has been preserved in its most pristine state, such as in wild animal sanctuaries and nature preserves, it is both protected and made meaningful by cultural intervention and so is no longer what it was for those who originally encountered it. Nonetheless, the experiences of those who first made this land a part of its inhabitants' cultural memory exist within symbolic meaning as traces of those origins that carry forward in time.

In the sense that Dewey gives to symbols and symbolic communication, our shared material world provides an unbroken connection to our past that runs through culture. However, even though culture carries old meaning into the future, in the present we constantly add to it meaning generated by our own experiences, and this new meaning interacts with the old. Thus symbolic meaning accumulates but also changes as symbols move from past to future. Culture is a rolling stone that *does* gather moss.

For example, in the Bordeaux region of France, you will find many artifacts of our cliff-dwelling, cave-painting ancestors, the Cro Magnon. Bone, rock, and flint tools found in the area reveal that these early *Homo sapiens sapiens* were our equal in their capacity to invent technology and create art, although their cultures lacked the rich heritage Cro Magnon and their descendants bequeathed to us. Yet even today, thousands of years later, we find traces of their culture in our own as we build, layer by layer, upon the social, technological, economic, political, and, in cases where humans continue to occupy their dwelling sites, even the physical structures they left behind. We cherish their material traces by studying, collecting, and visiting them in museums, just as we keep their memories alive in the myths and legends we tell our children about their ancestors.

Taking a dynamic view of culture, everything we can know or do is in the process of becoming part of our culture, such that culture changes ceaselessly. Take our knowledge of the Cro Magnon. Things like the paintings these early humans left on cave walls provide only the slimmest clues to their lives and thoughts, and we change our account of their history with each newly uncovered pile of artifacts. Thus the facts of history change over time as new interpretations of objects and events arise in the context of what was, at the time they were created, a distant and unknowable future.

As Dewey pointed out and Geertz confirmed, culture intertwines material and meaning and catches us up within its continuous change. A literary example may help. *Hamlet* read a second time is not the same text you encountered when you first read *Hamlet* because this twice-read *Hamlet* is infused with memories and emotions from your previous reading. All the material of the world is similarly altered by the meanings we make with it and, conversely, our meaning-making alters the material world. And because meaning is always in flux due to our ongoing experience of the material world, the latter can no more be fixed than can the former.

What things mean, and what meaning does to things, interpenetrate experience to shape us along with our culture as old cultural meaning leaks into new cultural material and old symbols are re-interpreted using new meanings. In this way, the cultural forces of material and meaning combine to produce the thread from which assumptions, values, artifacts, and symbols are spun, only to be woven back into culture by interacting humans whose identities are caught up within the webs of significance they continue to spin as they go about living, incessantly making more meaning and more artifacts.

Our identities are part of the material and meaning that constitute culture, just as they are products of that culture. Let's look into the dynamics of individual identity for insight into how organizational identity forms, is maintained, and changes.

## Identity and organizing

One of Dewey's close colleagues, social psychologist George Herbert Mead (1863–1931), understood identity to be intertwined with the cultural context that shapes individuals into selves. Mead proposed thinking of identity as a conversation between 'I' and 'me' that begins in infancy and continues throughout life (Figure 19a). Mead observed that 'me' comes into existence first, which happens when a child hears things about itself from others ('You have the cutest little nose,' 'You're getting so big!') and takes ownership of them ('my nose,' 'my size'). The act of owning one's 'me,' according to Mead, brings forth 'I.' From this moment

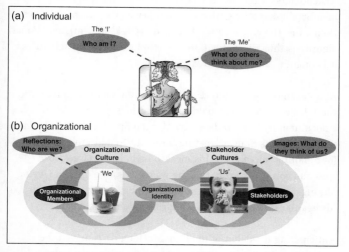

19. **Identity dynamics in a) individuals and b) organizations**

on, 'I' reacts to 'me,' and vice versa as each influences the other throughout life.

Of course, in the process of helping you form your identity, your conversation partners engage their own identity dynamics. My image of you influences your identity, which in turn reflects images of me back to my identity. This intertwining of identity construction processes provides an important foundation for the collective identity conversation that creates organizational identity.

Compared to individual identity, organizational identity conversations typically involve far greater complexity due to the number of people likely to be involved. Even so, the dynamics are similar (Figure 19b). However, for organizations the conversation occurs between 'us' (the organizational equivalent of 'me') and 'we' (the organizational equivalent of 'I'). 'Us' is constructed in numerous interactions with and among stakeholders, while 'we' emerges from organizational members' interactions with one another as they respond to 'us.' Defined as the conversation between 'us' and 'we,' organizational identity is thus distributed among employees and stakeholders; it is ongoing and multi-directional.

As an example of one direction a continuing identity conversation can take, consider McDonald's response to *Super Size Me*, a documentary film produced by Morgan Spurlock in 2004. The film documents Spurlock eating three McDonald's meals a day for a month, 'supersizing' his meal to include the largest size fries and soft drink every time he was offered the option. During filming, Spurlock gained 25 pounds amid growing concern for his health expressed by both his girlfriend and his doctor.

Anticipating the debut of the film, McDonald's removed the supersize option at its company-owned franchises and began a series of marketing campaigns to convince stakeholders of its commitment to healthy lifestyles. This effort included launching a line of salads. These and likeminded actions indicate that stakeholder images affected McDonald's 'us' prompting responses from its 'we.' But identity dynamics continue, promising to bring further change amid ongoing debate about the company and its involvement in the movement to reduce the threat of obesity throughout the world.

Other directions the identity conversation at McDonald's take involve different stakeholders. Some of these defend McDonald's, for example as a beloved brand or as a symbol of the consumer's right to choose. McDonald's 'we' responds to its fans, just as it does to its critics. And although the company's initial identity management efforts may have been designed to prevent any fundamental change in the way McDonald's operates (e.g. critics complain that its 'healthy' menu items still register extremely high calorie counts), even resistance to outside influence brings something new to its 'we.'

As you can see in the complexity of McDonald's organizational identity conversation there is no reason to expect either stakeholder images or the 'us' that emerges from them to be consistent. An exquisite new corporate headquarters building may favorably impress prospective investors ('they must be generating great wealth to afford such a wonderful facility'), customers ('such opulence indicates a great brand'), and community leaders ('what a marvelous aesthetic complement to the community'), while simultaneously being viewed as irresponsible by union leaders ('that money could have gone to increasing our wages') and environmentalists ('a little less squandering on executive perks and more environmental projects might have been possible').

Generically, the organizational identity conversation (Figure 19b) goes something like this: the organization collects stakeholder images using media analysis and market research techniques including reading blogs and following twitter, while other images are communicated directly via customer feedback during sales and service encounters or other interactions with members of the organization. The organization's 'us' forms around thoughts and feelings organizational members experience in regard to the identity they see in the mirror held up by stakeholders. Reflection on 'us' then engages the organization's culture and any subcultures that provide context for interpreting the images 'us' presents. If the 'us' confirms the 'we,' there will be no incentive to change. But disconfirmation calls for a change in response.

Over time, the conversation allows outside influence to change the organization's identity. This is because, regardless of whether reflection on 'us' produces confirmation or disconfirmation, organizational members respond to outsiders and in expressing who they are and what they stand for in relation to what others bring to the conversation, open themselves to change. Their responses may be intentional (e.g. advertising) or unintentional (e.g. through unscripted service encounters), but either way the responses organizational members make continue the conversation by leaving impressions on stakeholders inviting them to adapt their images and provide further feedback, which in turn opens culture to change.

Because the parties to an organizational identity conversation bring their cultural contexts with them, the organization's culture engages with the cultures of its stakeholders. This opening of cultures to each other makes change possible in the organization's culture as well as the cultures of stakeholders. Thus identity dynamics reveals how culture changes in response to external influence and vice versa.

This suggests that the missing piece of Schein's culture theory – external adaptation – can be provided by organizational

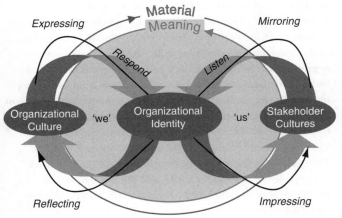

**20. Model combining organizational identity with cultural dynamics**

identity dynamics. In Figure 20, I have attempted to model this by incorporating the processes of material and meaning, described by Dewey, into the identity dynamics model. In the figure, culture and identity dynamics form a system of mutual influence fueled by the intertwining of material and meaning.

## Complexity, emergence, and networking

According to systems theory, a system has properties as a whole that cannot be traced to any of its component parts but instead arise from their interaction, for example as organizational identity arises from cultural members interacting with external stakeholders. Known as emergence, this phenomenon occurs in systems at all levels. One implication of emergence is that analyzing their components will never provide us with understanding adequate to control the complex systems we create by organizing. The behavior of complex systems can always surprise us and thus creates risk.

Sociologist Charles Perrow (1925– ) documented the risks of complex systems by studying what he ominously called normal accidents – failures such as the 1979 partial core meltdown of the nuclear reactor at Three Mile Island in Pennsylvania. Perrow showed how interactions between components of the technical systems controlling the reactor made it impossible to deduce the cause of the problem in time to intervene. A series of mechanical failures thus interacted with human limitations to produce near disaster. In 1986, the operators of the Chernobyl nuclear facility in Ukraine were not as fortunate. The explosions that occurred after Chernobyl's reactor vessel ruptured led to radioactive fallout and the evacuation and resettlement of over 300,000 people across Ukraine, Belarus, and Russia.

While historical analyses such as Perrow's may explain the behavior of complex systems in retrospect, they cannot predict the next surprise a complex system may have in store. For example, nothing prepared BP for the trouble they would face in bringing the oil spill in the Gulf of Mexico under control during the summer of 2010. In the face of system complexity and emergence, human limitations carry with them much risk, particularly within the context of globalization that includes multi-organizational partnerships such as BP's with Halliburton and Transocean.

BP's partnership illustrates that organizations change their configurations as global business stretches to encompass the world. Changes are also afoot for workers as old economy manufacturing jobs disappear or are outsourced, pushing workers into the new economy's service and knowledge/ information sectors. In the new economy, relationships between workers and organizations change too. Most participants in the new economy work freelance for multiple employers. They participate in temporary projects or create start-up firms, most of which do not last beyond a year or two. As they flit between

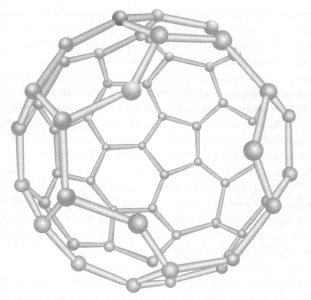

**21. Nodes and ties produce a network. Missing connections produce structural holes**

projects and employers, they replace their relationships to traditional organizations with professional and/or friendship networks.

Like any other social system, social networks *can* be depicted as static webs of interconnection on a graph showing links (ties) between participants known as actors (nodes). Actors can be defined as individuals or entire organizations (including different networks) or some combination of these. In addition to information and knowledge transfer, networks support the exchange of ideas, influence, energy, money, products, employment opportunities, and even culture. Access to these assets and capabilities is distributed such that no single individual or organization produces network outcomes alone, rather the network itself is the producer and provider.

Networks can emerge from traditional organizations as the result of outsourcing and supply chain management, or from partnerships or joint ventures. Benetton, for example, is comprised of hundreds of small clothing manufacturers and thousands of franchised sales outlets arrayed around a central distribution channel that provides a common information and control system and centralized marketing and finance functions. Many of the manufacturers joined Benetton because their small size would otherwise have prevented their participation in the international fashion market, and the sales outlets benefit from awareness of the Benetton brand and customer loyalty to it.

Benetton network partners are linked by an internalized free-market system where goods are bought and sold between them. This arrangement creates competitive pressures on the supplying partners to keep downward pressure on prices while it coordinates activities without needing much vertical hierarchy, which reduces administrative overhead. These characteristics reduce overall costs and increase the efficiency and profitability of the network. However, simple economic relationships between Benetton's partners could lead to exploitation.

Network partners might use the power they derive from controlling critical resources (e.g. access to capital, ability to design successful products) to influence decisions about profit distributions. Or, once the network as a whole generates demand for products, suppliers of the most popular items could withhold their contributions until their partners agree to pay them higher prices. In these situations, one part of the network could hold the rest hostage for a larger share of profits. Whereas bureaucracy would have been the response to such efforts in the old economy, the politics of networking appear to emerge, at least in some instances, differently.

The potential for political behavior pushes network partners like those of Benetton to develop more than economic interdependence. For instance, relationships built on friendship, reputation, shared culture, identity, or a corporate brand, enjoy greater cooperation and trust, and fewer attempts at domination. Thus one of the challenges in managing network relationships is building organizational cultures and brands to provide a shared sense of purpose and community without losing the benefits of diversity, overly restricting individual self-expression, or denying self-interest.

As it turns out, the politics of human behavior require carefully balancing networks between too much closure and so much openness that their identity becomes incoherent. Tight networks comprised of people who interact mainly with each other (e.g. cliques) differ from larger networks with looser ties that open themselves more readily to outside influence. There appears to be a tradeoff between the benefits of tight and open networks. Trust may be higher with those who do not surprise you, but innovation will be lower. Compared to members of tight networks, members of open networks enjoy a greater amount of new information, opportunity, and innovation due to their wider exposure to the ideas of others and open networks are also more likely to enjoy the advantages of diversity.

While openness spreads information and thereby enhances and disseminates innovation, it can make it difficult to profit from network activities in the same way that closed systems can. This leads some open networks to redefine the role of competition in social relationships, as open sourced computer software demonstrates. But it can also produce innovative business models demonstrated by IBM's solutions for a smarter planet initiative. IBM uses the smarter planet initiative to find new uses for its products and services by working in partnership with communities to solve their problems.

Today networking has become commonplace due to social media platforms offered by websites like Facebook, LinkedIn, and twitter that permit people to communicate as often as they like, including moment-to-moment about everything from 'what are you doing now?' to 'what are we doing here?' They re-establish and develop connections between old friends as well as facilitate meeting new people who might be located anywhere in the world. To the extent that users restrict access to their profiles and thoughts, they move the network in the direction of being closed, to the extent they continually link to new contacts, they open the networks as they circulate information about themselves and others.

Anyone can instantly disseminate relevant information throughout any electronically mediated network in which they participate, and links between networks move information rapidly in multiple directions at once, a phenomenon many describe as going viral, an epidemiological metaphor. Marketing provides one example of the organizational changes social networking brings. As marketers increase their use of social media to gain access to the networks in which their consumers participate, they move away from expensive and less easily targeted advertising campaigns. But access is a two-way street, and social media give stakeholders more opportunities to engage and influence organizations.

Networks encourage information sharing by granting status to those who share what they know instead of hoarding it. This produces a different power dynamic than that typical of hierarchical relationships. Instead of hierarchical positions of authority allocating power, network actors gain influence by occupying central node positions. Centrality in networks of influence provides the ability to connect others, acquire information, and use social capital, all of which translate into power. The difference is that, in networks, the power of particular nodes can shift rapidly. If one node is blocked or inactive, ties between other nodes permit the flow to be rerouted.

The ease of substituting one node for a neighbor means that the formal authoritative power of hierarchy subsides. In networks, most, if not all, vertical communication and control relationships are replaced with lateral relationships. Partnership becomes the norm, which is what makes life in networks appear to be more democratic than in other forms of organizing, though it is a democracy only in the sense that networks demand the participation of their members. This demand can be as oppressive as it is in any other organizational form, and perhaps more so due to the pressure it puts on individuals to stay connected all the time. But then, no form of organizing guarantees democracy. As with any other collective outcome, democracy rests with the uses to which organizing is put.

So far, focusing on organizing processes as opposed to organization(s) as entities has meant looking into what actors do in the context of their organizing activities. But some of the latest ideas about how organizing happens turn our attention away from actors to focus exclusively on actions and more particularly on interactions. Organization researcher Barbara Czarniawska (1948– ), for example, promotes the idea of action nets as opposed to actor networks. Action nets interweave actions with things acted upon (objects, relationships, words, meaning) forming shifting patterns that cannot hold one shape long enough to be called an organization. If organization does not disappear altogether, it remains only as a shadowy shapeshifter.

Many resist the idea that the emergence and growth of networks alongside other new economy developments means that formal organizations are disappearing. After all, corporations have never been bigger or more powerful than they are today. Furthermore, members of social networks often look for ways to meet face to face, suggesting there are limits to how far networking can go toward replacing more static organizations.

Others challenge the newness of networking. After all, grapevines and rumor mills demonstrate that networks have been with us for a long time. Although we may be entering an era when we find networks better suited to our immediate needs and desires than are more permanent configurations, this may not always be true. The pendulum could yet swing back to order and stability, reaffirming the view that organizations can be usefully depicted as entities.

# Chapter 6
# Where do we go from here?

Some pundits predict organizations will soon outsource nearly all their activity, leaving behind only a shell of their former corporate selves. Many manufacturing activities in the industrial organizations of the West have already been outsourced, leaving executives to oversee managers who supervise consultants who hire workers on a temporary basis to do the remaining work. The consultants, in turn, work for global service organizations supported by networks of scientists, engineers, and other knowledge workers operating via proprietary intranet servers.

You can easily imagine these business models morphing, through crowdsourcing, hacking, and other emergent activities, into a platform for organizing the work of anonymous freelancers who are contracted and paid on a project-by-project basis, much as craftworkers were in pre-industrial economies. Freelancers can find projects, submit work, and receive pay, all over computer-monitored electronic devices connected to the internet permitting networks to operate 24/7 from locations spread all over the Earth, and one day maybe beyond. As these changes take hold, traditional old economy organizations recede into the background or disappear altogether.

But as some organizations disappear, others emerge. For example, new kinds of employee unions offer freelancers group rates on health insurance and other benefits, and organize quasi office parties to fill the social needs created by the isolation, alienation, and fragmentation of working conditions typical in the emerging new economy. At the same time, various actors within the institutional environment of global business are organizing around a perceived need to control the biggest corporations, mainly by forming NGOs or joining global social movements to save the planet, eradicate poverty, or fight for human rights. Some say that the mix-and-match pastiche of the conditions of work life in the new economy coupled with reorganization of the institutional environment will reshape organizations rather than leading to their demise.

What comes next is a matter of speculation. Some ideas are wilder than others with some of the wildest coming from science fiction and metaphysics. This final chapter will draw on contrasts between old and new economy thinking to follow several quite different lines of conjecture concerning where organizing might be headed, or how we might evolve along with organizations.

## NGOs, social movements, and organizing as perpetual change

One interesting development emerging alongside NGOs and social movements is the recognition that whole human beings create, operate, and interact with organizations. Regarding humans holistically means acknowledging that, along with self-interest, humans have interests in society as well as in the organizations with which they engage as employees and/or stakeholders. Individuals who express their societal interests while at work push organizations (back) into the role of servant to society or to humankind, as opposed to being merely vehicles for expressing the economic and technological interests of the most powerful. This is what some people hope will be the consequence of the shift from industrial (old economy) to post-industrial (new economy) societies.

I have drawn four pictures representing the shifting roles organization(s) and organizing play as post-industrial society emerges. Figure 22 shows how, in this transition, the boundaries that defined traditional organizations, such as manufacturing firms, universities, or government agencies, reform around the activities and interests of people who contribute their energy, action, influence, culture, and capital to a joint enterprise.

The triangle in panel 22.1 represents organization-as-entity doing the traditional work of producing goods and services in the old economy. The many small gray blobs are various stakeholders, some of which have direct access to the organization indicated by their position inside the triangle. These latter blobs are owners, managers, employees, and any customers directly served by the

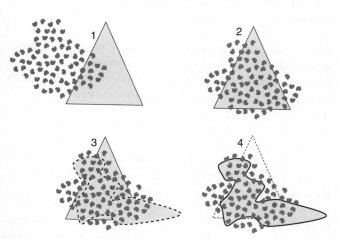

22. How organizational boundaries reform in the shift from industrial to post-industrial society: 1) a traditional organization, 2) a traditional organization as increasing numbers of stakeholders gain access to its resources, 3) parts of the traditional organization reorganizing around interests shared by employees and other stakeholders, and 4) these realignments solidified into one or more new and probably temporary organizations while the traditional organization melts into the background

organization's activities. Stakeholders positioned outside the boundaries of the triangle are interested in other outcomes, for example, the organization's environmental or social impact, or its ethics.

In panel 2, more and more stakeholder interests have been taken into account inside the organization by its different functions – marketing to serve customers, HR to serve employees, finance to serve the capital markets, PR to handle media and community relations, and so on. As time passes the relationships forged between insiders and outsiders give outsiders access to the organization, bringing them within its walls to engage actively in co-creation with organizational employees. This is occurring today in organizations like LEGO Group that create new products and train new employees with the help of LEGO users who volunteer as product designers or help train new employees.

When you compare panels 22.1 and 22.2, you see change in the invasion of the organization by many more blobs. For a time, the purposes of the panel 2 organization may become befuddled by the influence of so many competing interests attracted by the appeal of engagement or the attractions of co-creation, an effect compounded by the organization's pursuit of legitimacy in the eyes of these stakeholders. If corporate interests prevail, the organization will return to the state depicted in panel 1 by resisting pressure to adapt to the new economy. Alternatively, the scenario shown in panel 22.3 unfolds.

In panel 22.3, it becomes difficult to differentiate employees from other actors as stakeholder engagement provides greater access to the internal workings and resources of the organization. As this happens, whole human beings act on both organizational and extra-organizational interests. In some cases, for example, ethics becomes a key concern and produces a new business model that is less focused on doing well (e.g. making a profit) then on doing good (i.e. serving society). New boundaries emerge within and around the triangle in panel 3 as stakeholders align with employees around common interests and together engage in activities supporting them with corporate resources and capabilities (e.g. by providing manpower and/or management).

IBM's Corporate Service Corp provides an example. IBM Service Corp volunteers serve the corporate vision of creating a smarter planet by living in an impoverished community they pledge to serve for six to twelve months. There they take on projects co-designed with locals to apply the technologies and services that IBM then delivers to solving the community's most urgent problems. A critic might see this only as an attempt by IBM to grow its market, but from the point of view of community members, it is an opportunity to take advantage of the resources and capabilities of this massive corporation. From IBM's point of view, it is one means of generating business model innovation as the volunteers serve its grand ambition to create a 'smarter planet.' Panel 22.3 shows how, as insiders and outsiders join forces, the boundaries of an organization like IBM's start to shift, reshaping its identity.

If alliances between society and business, such as those encouraged by the IBM Corporate Service Corp, were to become institutionalized then one more shift would occur. In panel 23.4, the solidified yet organic shape of the boundary around the aligned stakeholder interests depicts a new form of organizing emerging from the older form whose now dotted boundary indicates its potential disappearance. And of course the changes depicted by all the panels of Figure 22 are or will be ricocheting throughout the global economy, co-occurring and intermingling all over the planet to create conditions for further complexity and emergence.

If organizing continues to produce emergent properties, institutionalization will become less and less likely. The new boundaries shown in panel 22.4 will not hold and organizing as depicted by the organic shape in the center of panel 22.3 along with the disappearing boundary around formal organization in panel 22.4 will prevail. In this scenario, temporary organizations (or rather organizings) emerge from and melt back into networks whose boundaries are never clear for long even as a few old economy organizations persist, albeit as shells serviced by new economy freelancers. This does not mean, however, that the cultural, identity, or power dynamics of people working together will cease, only that the temporary nature of organizing will replace our static appreciations (e.g. structure) with a more liquid view.

## Culture, spirit, and the new physics of hyperspace

Long ago Karl Marx predicted that at some point in the development of capitalism the superstructure of modern politics, culture, art, religion and philosophy would float free of its economic base of technologically driven production. Statements like 'all that is solid melts into air' somehow ring truer now that Soviet style communism has collapsed than they did when Marx first criticized capitalism. It took much longer than he imagined, but as we confront virtual organizations, networking, crowdsourcing, hacking, and other emergent phenomena reshaping the globalizing economy, we may need to reassess Marx's ideas about the changing relationship between economies and culture, religion, art, politics, and philosophy. Let's follow this idea into culture and spirituality.

Organizing, with or without organization(s), will continue in the ether of the internet and as it does, cultural processes will cross over into and territorialize cyberspace. You can see this taking shape in the norms and expectations set forth as part of membership in many web-based communities, such as the virtual world created by Linden Lab known as Second Life. Second Life's residents interact through avatars they create and control. Not only are residents expected to adhere to certain virtual world rules of conduct, there are real world laws to be followed as well (e.g. no offensive activity or language, no gambling, no copyright infringement). Or consider the strict rules created and followed by those who write and edit entries for Wikipedia's electronic encyclopedia. It is clear that culture is alive and well in these virtually organized venues.

But cyberspace is practically pure symbolism. It seems likely that culture will become an even more powerful force than it was in the old economy because its symbolic character matches the emergent properties of the new economy. Just notice the extent to which markets now value businesses as much if not more for their brands as for the functionality of their products and services, or how brand fan bases grow beyond consumer groups into worldwide virtual communities. Think about the emerging role the Internet plays in political fundraising that allows the combined strength of small contributors to create new avenues to democracy. Or think about what will draw freelancers and fans to the websites that will engage them in the future and attract the resources they command – is it more likely to be the need to earn a living or will it be earning a living doing something meaningful and/or fun?

For the moment, networks are altering cultures faster than culture is developing within or around networks, but this will probably not always be the case. As humans adapt to new economic conditions, their actions will produce culture along with the emergent processes brought about by their organizing. Culture is produced by all instances of human contact – it just takes different shapes depending on who is interacting, where and why (e.g. businesses versus freelancers' unions versus rallies, marches, and flash mobs). Culture may not require the static structures of old economy organizations to survive and maybe it will even thrive in newfound freedom from the institutional pressures to conform that restrict creativity and innovation.

One possibility to consider is that all the changes underway are happening in our perceptions or to our consciousness, making us more sensitive to dynamic forces of power, culture and identity that were there all along but hidden from our view. Systems theory implies that social organizations are a special case for us because people are key components from which they emerge. Participation in these systems provides us with an insider's view of organizational emergence (i.e. organizing), but deprives us of an overview of the system as a whole (i.e. the social organization as an entity). It's a future we dare not try to control because our ability to understand it is so limited.

The new physics developing out of the theory of relativity, quantum mechanics and string theory, offers the notion of hyperspace as an intriguing way of understanding organizing as cultural experience. Hyperspace is any space of a dimension greater than three, starting with spacetime, which includes the three spatial dimensions of height, width, and depth, plus time. What the extra dimensions beyond these four might be is a matter of speculation, but schoolteacher E. A. Abbott (1838–1926) made a persuasive case in *Flatland: A Romance in Many Dimensions* that any creature of n-dimensions will experience the n+1 dimension as existing inside itself. At the systems level of social organization, the dimension that lies within might well be what we know as our culture.

Einstein's theory of relativity included the principle of the curvature of space-time, which implies that gravity forces light to bend, a phenomenon that has since been proven by scientific experimentation. One popular way of explaining what this discovery means in human terms is to note that, if we were able to look far enough forward in spacetime, we would end up looking at the back of our own heads. What does this imply about the positions we take in the world that define our ways of seeing as well as what we (think we) know? Would it be possible to look beyond the back of our heads and glimpse what lies over our shoulders?

Metaphorically speaking, looking over our own shoulders is more or less what we do when we glimpse culture and come to understand its symbolism, social construction, and sensemaking processes. Keeping our shoulder in view reminds us that we are bound to a unique subjective position even though it is one that looks out on a larger reality we share with others who are similarly bound to their unique locations within the whole. This uniqueness explains the intersubjectivity required to access culture, we cannot experience it unless we engage with other cultural members. Might intersubjectivity position us to explore the fifth dimension lying within our collective consciousness?

Combining the new physics with dynamic ways of thinking about the three Os suggests we always confront our past as we create our future in the momentary present of our existence. Culture manifests our heritage by inserting its vestiges into contemporary life, not unlike the idea of spacetime bending back on itself, an idea that provokes much speculation about time travel. Some physicists are convinced that jumps between two temporal points brought into proximity by the furrowed surface of five-dimensional space could allow for time travel. Could cultural intersubjectivity furrow individual awareness such that we might leap from our own narrow understanding to empathy with another cultural member or even with the whole?

Given that culture allows us to symbolically align with our origins, as when we share stories of our ancestors or contemplate the artifacts they left to us, could it be that these intersubjective experiences constitute and/or grant access to a five-dimensional space whose contours form and are formed by our cultural heritage? Literature shows us that stories can transport us somewhere beyond the limits of ordinary consciousness, as do dreams and religious experiences. Some spiritual leaders, such as the Dalai Lama, have noted the striking similarity between the territory spirituality opens and ideas being explored by the new physics of hyperspace. As far as can be told from the archeological record left by the Cro Magnon, culture and religion originated together – why should they not work together now to help us confront the future?

## The art and craft of organizing: design aesthetics and jazz

Thoughts about culture as hyperspace make me curious about how humans expand their consciousness when they coordinate their interests, intentions, and activities with those of others. What happens to their thoughts, feelings, and aesthetic sensibilities when they engage in the processes from which social organization emerges? How do these changes affect intersubjectivity and how is human organizing altered by it?

In psychology, empathy refers to tapping into someone else's emotional state, literally feeling what they feel. Directed toward an entire organization, empathy would need to resonate with the collective experience of a group of people or society as a whole, rather than that of one individual. It is a capacity the best artists of any generation seem to master and it is probably what allows us to see ourselves in and thus appreciate great art. Designers also cultivate social empathy to innovate new products, services, or brand experiences that appeal to a great many potential users.

Could social empathy developed within the practices of art and design explain how we tacitly grasp the rich and nuanced web of significance that defines our cultural context? Seen in this way, cultural and identity dynamics might be thought of as an empathic exercise directed not at one other human, but at the experience of multiple humans intersubjectively organizing their purposeful activities through shared sensemaking, enactment, and social construction processes. By aesthetically and emotionally as well as intellectually participating in the co-construction of meaning, humans may open themselves to a broad web of cultural understanding in the same way artists and designers gain inspiration for their work.

For me, organizing resonates more with the arts than does organization because institutions are too rigid to support the revolutionary change that the best artistic practices celebrate. This is why many artists resist all forms of societal expectation and often do their best work before they come into contact with museums and other arts establishments. Nonetheless, organizing is what artists must do to create art, whether it involves assembling material in the visual arts, movement in dance, sound in music, or all three in theatre. As these artistic examples suggest, organizing is performing.

Throughout their history, managers and organizational researchers have given performance more attention than any other topic. Definitions of organizational performance traditionally referred to results, such as production quantities, sales revenue, profit, and return on investment (ROI). Performing artists define performance quite differently as actions taken to express a feeling, sensation, thought, or idea. What if we redefined organizational performance along these artistic lines?

What if members of organizations returned to the roots of designing and producing products, which lie in the applied arts of craftsmanship? *Techne* is the Greek root of our modern words technical and technology but, in contrast to contemporary meanings, ancient Greeks used this term to refer to the skill of the artist. Of course, en route from artists in ancient Greece to modern times, the meaning of *techne* was reshaped by artisans of the Middle Ages, by craftworkers in the pre-industrial era, and by engineers and designers in the industrial age.

Today, modern applications of science to engineering and manufacturing have largely overshadowed ancient links between technology and art that culminated in the works of Leonardo da Vinci (1452–1519). Modern technology is equated with its most objective features – the tools, equipment, machines, and procedures through which work is accomplished. But its links to a past in applied and other arts remain available within the organizational cultures that carry *techne*'s trace.

Changes afoot in the new economy of post-industrialism can bring the past close again. For example, while Nissan's latest brand slogan calls on us to 'Shift_' our thinking about the company, inside Nissan things are shifting, too, as art and craftsmanship reclaim territory once lost to more purely industrial understandings of technology. The presence of marketing specialists on product development teams, for instance, provokes new approaches to designing a car. One result of the involvement of marketers is that, Nissan's Japanese heritage is now symbolized around the world by the ancient calligraphic line that traces a graceful arc through all its car designs. This line subtly unites the company's past with the futuristic world it invites you to enter whenever you visit one of its many shiny new dealer showrooms or drive one of its restyled cars.

One of my favorite metaphors for bringing the artistry of organizing into the open is jazz. Not just as a form of improvisation, but also in the way jazz players, like other musicians, make music through a complex and multi-layered use of organizing skills. Like all musicians, those who play jazz not only perform technically on their instruments, they must also train themselves in the complex language of music, and learn how to put a band of musicians together.

Jazz bands are mainly organized around gigs. When there is work, the player who got the gig makes a choice of other musicians to invite depending upon the audience expected (e.g. jazz fans, people who want to dance, people seeking a certain ambiance for conversation), the number of players needed (e.g. a duo or trio, a four- or five-piece, big band or jazz orchestra), the mix of instruments desired (e.g. the 'voices' of bass, drums, keyboard, trumpet, sax, vocalist), the local players available, and so on.

Once a group is selected to play a gig the musicians must coordinate their interactions to perform a set of tunes that engages their audience without causing any unnecessary animosity on stage, and hopefully creating some original music. This they do within the barest structural outlines of the tunes they will play and do not necessarily choose tunes until they are in the context of the performance. They improvise tunes around minimal structures known as 'heads.'

When they are playing well, jazz musicians listen and respond to one another each and every moment they perform. The feat of jazz performance, given all the organizing required both before and during the gig, makes jazz music an example for organizations faced with continuous rapid change. Moreover, improvisation opens a space for the fluid and emergent properties of organizing to achieve satisfaction and value for those who participate in its transitory forms.

Before the Enlightenment, nearly all music was improvisational. And while jazz is the most recent improvisational musical genre to appear, there is a movement to embrace free improvisation developing among other types of musicians. Could this development be evidence that we humans always work backwards as we move forward in time, reclaiming threads from a past reaching at least to the Cro Magnon as we construct our future?

Regardless of whether you see the future of organizations in terms of returning to what worked in the past, or pressing into new territory, it is safe to assume that humans will survive only in so far as they continue to organize. If change comes too fast for organizing processes to ever again settle into predictable routines, then humans will have to constantly invent new ways to coordinate their activities and agree upon how to use the resources this or some other planet provides. In doing this, they will doubtless continue to draw upon culturally embedded beliefs as they face uncertainties and grapple with power, improvising the coordination required to set and achieve their goals.

By reading this book, you have been introduced to many different ways to think and talk about organizations. I hope that you will find among the ideas presented some that are useful to you as you engage in organizing your and our future. If you are interested in learning more about the backgrounds of the people and ideas mentioned in this book, please keep reading. The Appendix will introduce you to the field of organization theory and some of the different foundations organizational scholars have drawn upon to produce the knowledge presented here. It will deepen your understanding of organizations to appreciate the contexts within which their knowledge developed and perhaps inspire you to join them in the continuing study of organization(s) and organizing.

# Appendix

# Why organizational scholars disagree: politics and philosophy

Organization theory is a mutt of a discipline. Perhaps because social organization emerges at a higher level of complexity and understanding than that of humans, organizational scholars find themselves searching other disciplines for answers to questions about organization(s) and organizing. In addition to organization theory, ideas explored in this book came from economics and engineering, sociology, psychology, and anthropology, literature, philosophy, and the arts. This degree of interdisciplinarity brings with it many disagreements and you have no doubt sensed some of them in the variety of ideas offered to explain the three Os. This Appendix examines some of the reasons why topics of organization(s) and organizing inspire so much contention.

## Objectivism versus interpretivism

Ontology refers to any philosophical examination of what it means to exist. It calls forth assumptions about being and in this sense determines what can be said to exist. For example, some people believe in the existence only of that which can be perceived with the five senses, while others claim that anything to which a noun refers exists. Epistemology, the theory of knowledge, tackles issues of truth, belief, and justification. It involves answering questions such as 'what is knowledge?' and 'how do we know,' for instance, that this or that exists?

One of the earliest points of contention concerning organizations arose from competing preferences for either ontology or epistemology. Objectivists, who typically start with ontology, believe something exists only to the extent that it can be verified through independent (i.e. objective) observation. Independent means that different people, all having the same relationship to an object, make similar observations about it. Their observations should not be biased by their personal views or the context in which they are embedded. For hardcore objectivists, subjective understanding equates to personal bias that needs to be shed to establish the truth about the world as it exists.

Subjectivists put greater emphasis on epistemological than on ontological assumptions, believing that there are many phenomena that would be unknowable using the methods designed by and for objectivists. These include thoughts, feelings, and social processes like organizing that are difficult if not impossible to perceive using the five senses alone; they require the very subjectivity that objectivists want to dismiss. Social phenomena in particular (e.g. culture) would be unobservable if not for our capacity to experience and communicate intersubjectively. Furthermore, phenomena engaged subjectively are experienced differently depending on who is experiencing them and under what conditions they are perceived (e.g. good or bad mood, within one cultural context or another), therefore how we know (epistemology) influences what can be known, thus shaping our ontological assumptions about what exists.

In epistemological terms, interpretivism refers to the belief that knowledge is a matter of interpretation. Interpretivists emphasize that which is meaningful in social and cultural life and how meaning comes to be made and shared. Researchers working within interpretive traditions analyze the meanings people confer upon and thus use to organize their experiences. They typically take care not to impose their interpretations on others, but recognize at the same time the impossibility of fully understanding anyone else's experience.

If you believe that reality is objectively real, then you can develop positive knowledge about it by eliminating ideas that do not match observations that can be independently validated and reliably confirmed. But requirements for validity and reliability demanded for meeting the conditions of objectivity cannot be applied to inquiry into subjective phenomena because one would not expect two subjective experiences to be the same. As a result of their epistemological position, subjectivists cannot accept the institutionalized rules of the scientific method defined by objectivists if they are to study what they believe exists beyond the realm defined as objective. Subjectivists' efforts to redefine the rules of science push positivists to deeper reflection on their own position.

Positivism arose in ancient Greece and waxed and waned in popularity until philosopher August Comte (1798–1857), one of the founders of sociology, used it to replace metaphysics with the scientific method. Comte promoted a science based in observations of the world and saw theory as valuable to the extent that it could be empirically tested against the phenomena it explains.

Along with Marx and Weber, Émile Durkheim (1858–1917) helped to found the social sciences by applying positivism to statistical data he collected on suicides in France. Durkheim used his data to explain relationships between social context and individual acts of self-destruction. The mathematical appeal of his argument, along with his unexpected findings, inspired many others within the developing social sciences to employ positivist epistemology, eventually including organization studies. To this day, positivism rules the social as well as the physical sciences on which it is modeled.

However, these days most positivists admit that it is impossible to remove all bias from observation and that a uniquely correct solution to the problems studied by social scientists will likely never be found. This has weakened opinions that only positivist science is acceptable, and opened the door to interpretivism and other epistemological foundations for generating knowledge. It has also permitted positivists to claim that the differences between their epistemological position and that of the subjectivists are not so great, an argument some use to continue discrediting or ignoring interpretive research findings. According to most interpretivists, the weaker claim also maintains the dominance of the institutions of positivism, mainly those of mainstream science.

Beyond debating ontological assumptions and epistemological positions, there are choices to be made about how to study the phenomena they define. These methodological choices lead to further disagreements over how to conduct oneself as a researcher and what counts as data. For example, positivists like 'hard' data, such as numbers gleaned from financial records or taken from surveys of large samples of the organizational population under study or of an organization's members or stakeholders (e.g. employee or customer surveys). Interpretivists prefer 'soft' data, such as that produced by unstructured interviews or through participant observation of organizational members or their stakeholders as they engage in processes such as decision-making, teamwork, or networking.

There are traditional alignments between objective ontology and positivist epistemology and between subjectivist ontology and interpretive epistemology, but there is no necessity compelling these pairings. Other positions recombine these stances giving us, for example critical realism which is a blend of objectivist ontology and interpretive epistemology. Critical realists believe that although subjectivity presents itself in everything we know, this does not deny the objectively real. For them, subjectivity binds us to taking interpretation into account whenever we make an empirical study, but does not preclude us from making reference to that which (they believe) exists objectively.

While critical realists combine objective ontology and interpretive epistemology, others have fashioned alternatives outside ontological and epistemological domains altogether. For example, poststructuralists believe there can be no solid ground upon which to build any philosophy because the meaning of words is relative and constantly shifting. Postmodernism borrows this anti-foundational position and combines it with insights from the arts and humanities including especially literary theory and aesthetic philosophy, though some postmodernists ground themselves in architecture and the arts where the term 'postmodern' first appeared.

## The postmodern (linguistic) turn

Postmodernists take the position that the world is made by, rather than mirrored in, language. The world and everything in it is constituted and made real by language occurring within discourse. The subject position 'I' in a sentence beginning 'I am' constitutes my existence, just as talk about existence constitutes reality. There can be no reality or identity apart from that created in and by language because language gives us, and the things surrounding us, existence. This idea is anti-foundational in the sense that it pulls the rug out from under previous ontological assumptions and epistemological positions leaving philosophy without any permanent foundation. In postmodern ontology, things are created when we speak or write about them, that is, they exist linguistically, but only in text or discourse.

Postmodernism denies that words represent things. Our way of speaking constitutes our experience of reality. 'In the saying it comes to pass that the world is made to appear,' as Martin Heidegger put it. This turn toward language to explain reality began when Heidegger accused philosophers from Plato on of treating being as substantial, leading us astray by focusing our attention on things and their properties to the exclusion of that which produces our fixation on things, namely how we talk about them. Heidegger wanted to know what permitted being to show up as entities and concluded it is language and the discourses created by speaking, writing, and reading. Our ways of thereby linguistically constructing things is what gives them existence.

Postmodernists share several beliefs stemming from the linguistic turn. First, the discourses in which we engage shape our reality by influencing how we use language and what we talk about (e.g. the discourse of organizations versus that of organizing). Second, speaker, spoken, and speech are all constituted in and through language. Third, meaning cannot be fixed, nor can reality, they are always in flux, moving within and between discourses, potentially changing with each new utterance. And finally, there is no independent reality against which to test knowledge, all is text read or performed in the moment of continual becoming.

Power and communication are central to the critical position inspired by postmodernism because anyone who controls discourse can make something exist, or disappear. For example, maladies such as multiple sclerosis (MS) or attention-deficit hyperactivity disorder (ADHD) cannot be treated until they are given existence by being spoken about within a discourse (i.e. the discourse of medical practice). Power relations are present everywhere by virtue of institutionally legitimated expertise and/or the greater communicative abilities of some rather than others. Oppression and repression, for example, are communicative distortions arising from imbalances of power supported by ignorance of what produces reality. Emancipation from these social ills can be gained only through awareness of how language and discourse produce reality.

To see how language constructs reality, let's return to the metaphors of machine, organism, culture, and psychic prison with which we began. Each metaphor suggests and thereby produces a different understanding of organization(s) and organizing. This linguistic act is not merely a clever use of figurative language, it is language constituting us in a way that creates and legitimates different ideas about organization(s) and organizing.

When you adopt the machine metaphor, you face an organization constituted as an entity, a structure of decisions, actions and technological choices driven by rationality, efficiency and effectiveness all of which are defined relative to stated goals and purposes. The language of the machine and the idea of the engineer who designed or operates it plants images of designing and controlling the organization in your head and presents you with a vocabulary including 'design,' 'control,' and the image of an engineer/manager who 'drives' the machine/organization.

By contrast, the metaphor of the organism as a living system constitutes the organization as a 'system' comprised of 'subsystems' that are all part of an 'environment' that provides 'resources' enabling 'survival' and encouraging 'competition.' Alternatively, using the language of culture presents an organization that is shaped by its 'meanings' and processes of 'sensemaking' and 'social construction.' The 'symbolic order' or 'web of meaning' that informs thoughts about organizations as cultures contrasts sharply to the 'rational order' produced by 'hierarchy,' 'technological necessity' or 'environmental influence.'

Adopting the text metaphor of postmodernism turns the whole enterprise of language inward upon itself. Here, language does not just give us imagination for things, it gives us 'I,' 'you,' 'us.' Our language writes and rewrites us into the world we construct through language. It also suggests an escape route should we choose to take it.

Postmodernists offer us the option of joining forces by our participation in discourse. Doing so 'reflexively' – with awareness of the effects of language – permits change even if only in our self-conceptions. If we find organizing processes to be degrading, it is up to us to voice our concerns and thereby change the discursive reality we deplore. Criticizing organizations, for example by invoking the psychic prison metaphor, moves us toward emancipation.

## Thinking in process

Process philosophy is not anti-foundational so much as it abandons pursuit of stable philosophical foundations by embracing change as an alternative foundational assumption. Like postmodernism, it contrasts with essentialist philosophies that have dominated thought since the Enlightenment, but diverges with it by following a line of thought different to that set forth by Socrates and Plato.

For Socrates and Plato, everything had an essence such that, regardless of what happened to or around it, there was continuity of identity. For example, in spite of aging and the unfolding circumstances of your life, you are still you. This type of thinking favors a view of organization-as-entity. The opposing view of organizing-as-process arises from the belief that reality is change. Though organizational change has long been a subject of concern for managers, it has only been with the shift of preferences for organizing over organization(s) that organizational scholars have given process philosophy much attention.

Process philosophy brings with it an emphasis on becoming (e.g. focusing on enactment or social construction as they happen), as opposed to being (e.g. examining that which already is – an entity). It provides definitions of organizing based on what people are doing as they organize themselves. Where static definitions assume that organizations have properties that can be objectively observed and compared, the dynamic perspective of process philosophy assumes it is impossible to define organization because it is always on the way to becoming something other than what it was a moment ago.

The appropriate role of anyone interested in organizing is to engage in processes of organizational becoming so as to reveal how organization looks from within. But, to be convincing to someone standing outside of the dynamic under examination, methods of demonstration are more effective than description. The audience must be engaged in the process if they are to witness and thereby verify its existence or experience its significance. Demonstration is a performative act, you do rather than describe or explain, and, in doing with others, transfer some of your appreciation for both the act and its significance to them, even as some of their meaning and appreciation for your joint effort rubs off on you.

To conclude with one of my earlier and favorite points, process marks the difference between dead institutions and living culture. The former shows us organization(s) as finished works or beings, the latter invites us to experience organizing as it emerges and to engage in processes of collective becoming, even as our individual becoming inflects the collective process. Organizing makes it impossible to know organizations as entities or to separate our selves from our organizing. As the poet William Butler Yeats (1865–1939) famously put it:

> O chestnut-tree, great-rooted blossomer,
> Are you the leaf, the blossom or the bole?
> O body swayed to music, O brightening glance,
> How can we know the dancer from the dance?

We are made of and for organizing.

# References

## Chapter 1

The thinking that went into this book was informed by my writing of *Organization Theory: Modern, Symbolic and Postmodern Perspectives* (1997; 2nd edn. with A. Cunliffe, Oxford University Press, 2006), where you will find deeper discussions and further background on nearly all the topics you will read about here.

The material on the Tsukiji Fish Market is based on T. Bestor, *Tsukiji: The Fish Market at the Center of the World* (Berkeley, CA: University of California Press, 2004).

Arguably the two most important resources on the development of industrial capitalism are M. Weber, *The Protestant Ethic and 'The Spirit of Capitalism'*, tr. P. Baehr and G. C. Wells (London: Penguin Books, 2002) and K. Marx, *Capital: A Critique of Political Economy* (1867; in German as *Das Kapital*, ed. F. Engels and S. L. Levitsky; tr. B. Fowkes, London: Penguin Classics, 1990).

Stakeholder theory was first presented by R. E. Freeman in *Strategic Management: A Stakeholder Approach* (Boston, MA: Pitman, 1984).

G. Morgan, *Images of Organization* (1986; 2nd edn., Thousand Oaks, CA: Sage, 1997) is the classic reference on metaphors for organization. In addition to machine, organism, culture, and psychic prison, he offers the brain, complexity (flux and transformation), and instruments of domination. I combined domination with the psychic prison metaphor. Complexity is addressed in Chapter 5.

F. Taylor, *Principles of Scientific Management* (New York: Harper and Brothers, 1911).

General systems theory is usually traced to L. von Bertalanffy's 'An
  Outline of General Systems Theory', *British Journal for the
  Philosophy of Science*, 1, 2 (1950). The hierarchy of systems comes
  from K. Boulding, 'General Systems Theory: The Skeleton of a
  Science', *Management Science*, 2, 3 (April 1956): 197–208; find it
  online at http://www.panarchy.org/boulding/systems.1956.html
  accessed 11 November 2010.

C. Geertz, *The Interpretation of Culture* (New York: Basic Books, 1973).


## Chapter 2

Quotations from M. Weber, *Economy and Society: An Outline of
  Interpretive Sociology* (1956; G. Roth and C. Wittich (eds.),
  Berkeley, CA: University of California Press, 1978) will be found on
  pp. 975 and 987. The 'polar night of icy darkness' quotation can be
  found in P. Lassman (ed.), *Weber: Political Writings*
  (Cambridge, UK: Cambridge Texts in the History of Political
  Thought, 1994), p. xvi.

Quotation is from Plato, *The Republic* (360 BC; London: Penguin
  Classics, 1955), p. 103.

A. Smith, *An Inquiry into the Nature and Causes of the Wealth of
  Nations* (1776; http://socserv.socsci.mcmaster.ca/oldecon/ugcm/
  3ll3/smith/wealth/index.html, accessed 11 November 2010), see
  also D. Hume on the 'partition of employments' in *A Treatise of
  Human Nature* (1739; http://socserv2.socsci.mcmaster.ca/~econ/
  ugcm/3ll3/hume/treat.html, accessed 11 November 2010) and
  É. Durkheim, *On the Division of Labor in Society* (French, as
  *De la Division du Travail social*, 1893; tr. W. D. Halls, Free Press,
  1984).

H. D. Thoreau, *Walden; Or, Life in the Woods* (Boston, MA: Ticknor
  and Fields, 1854).

R. W. Emerson, 'The American Scholar' (speech delivered in 1837 to
  the Phi Beta Kappa Society in Cambridge, Massachusetts;
  http://www.emersoncentral.com/amscholar.htm, accessed 11
  November 2010).

J. Bentham, 'Panopticon' (http://cartome.org/panopticon2.htm,
  accessed 11 November 2010).

M. Heidegger, 'The Question Concerning Technology', in W. Lovitt's
  *The Question Concerning Technology and Other Essays* (New York:
  Harper Torchbooks, 1977), pp. 3–35.

C. Perrow, *Normal Accidents: Living with High Risk Technologies* (1984, Basic Books; Princeton, NJ: Princeton University Press, 1999).

J. Woodward, *Industrial Organization: Theory and Practice* (1965; New York: Oxford University Press, 1981).

P. Lawrence and J. Lorsch, *Organization and Environment: Managing Differentiation and Integration* (Cambridge, MA: Harvard University Press, 1967).

## Chapter 3

H. Garfinkel, *Studies in Ethnomethodology: Expanded and Updated Edition* (1967; Polity Press; Englewood Cliffs, NJ: Prentice-Hall, 2010).

P. Berger and T. Luckmann, *The Social Construction of Reality* (Garden City, NY: Anchor Books, 1966), p. 65.

Quotation is from W. I. Thomas and D. S. Thomas, *The Child in America: Behavior Problems and Programs* (New York: Knopf, 1928).

First Weick quotation is from p. 243 of the second edition of K. Weick, *The Social Psychology of Organizing* (New York: Addison-Wesley, 1979).

Second Weick quotation is from pp. 30–1 of K. Weick, *Sensemaking in Organizations* (Thousand Oaks, CA: Sage, 1995).

Two classic applications of institutional theory to organizations are J. Meyer and B. Rowan, 'Institutionalized Organizations: Formal Structure as Myth and Ceremony', *American Journal of Sociology*, 83 (1977), pp. 440–63, and L. Zucker, 'The Role of Institutionalization in Cultural Persistence', *American Sociological Review*, 42 (1977), pp. 726–43. On managers only seeming to be rational, see J. Pfeffer, 'Management as Symbolic Action: The Creation and Maintenance of Organizational Paradigms', in L. L. Cummings and B. M. Staw (eds.), *Research in Organizational Behavior*, Vol. 3 (Greenwich, CT: JAI Press, 1981), pp. 1–52.

On the invisible hand, see A. Smith, *An Inquiry into the Nature and Causes of the Wealth of Nations* (1776; http://socserv.socsci. mcmaster.ca/oldecon/ugcm/3ll3/smith/wealth/index.html, accessed 11 November 2010).

For markets and bureaucracy, see O. Williamson, *Markets and Hierarchies: Analysis and Antitrust Implications* (New York: Free

Press, 1975) and W. Ouchi, 'Markets, Bureaucracies, and Clans', *Administrative Science Quarterly*, Vol. 25 (1980): 129–41.

On social movements in relation to organizations, see H. Rao, C. Morrill, and M. N. Zald, 'Power Plays: How Social Movements and Collective Action Create New Organizational Forms', in B. Staw (ed.), *Research in Organizational Behavior*, Vol. 22 (Greenwich, CT: JAI Press, 2000), pp. 239–82.

The quotation from Geertz is found in C. Geertz, *The Interpretation of Culture* (New York: Basic Books, 1973), p. 5.

Schein's definition of organizational culture is E. Schein, *Organizational Culture and Leadership* (San Francisco, CA: Jossey-Bass, 1985), p. 6. One of his primary influences was the work of anthropologists F. R. Kluckhohn and F. L. Strodtbeck, *Variations in Value Orientations* (New York: HarperCollins, 1961).

P. Gagliardi, 'The Creation and Change of Organizational Cultures: A Conceptual Framework', *Organization Studies*, Vol. 7 (1986): 117–34.

J. Martin and C. Siehl, 'Organizational Culture and Counter Culture: An Uneasy Symbiosis', *Organizational Dynamics* (Fall 1983): 52–64.

J. Van Maanen and S. Barley, 'Occupational Communities: Culture and Control in Organizations', in B. M. Staw and L. L. Cummings (eds.), *Research in Organizational Behavior* (Greenich, CT: JAI Press, 1984), pp. 287–366.

## Chapter 4

A good place to begin reading about Karl Marx is P. Singer, *Marx: A Very Short Introduction* (Oxford: Oxford University Press, 2000). There you will also find many sources for further study depending upon your interests.

The definition of power as A's influence over B was first proposed by R. A. Dahl, 'The Concept of Power', *Behavioral Scientist*, Vol. 2 (1957): 202–15.

For more on the sources of individual power, see J. French and B. Raven, 'The Bases of Social Power', in D. Cartwright (ed.), *Studies in Social Power* (Ann Arbor, MI: University of Michigan Press, 1959).

David Mechanic, 'Sources of Power of Lower Participants in Complex Organizations', *Administrative Science Quarterly*, Vol. 7/3 (1962): 349–64 discusses the power of lower-level organizational members.

On bounded rationality and satisficing, as well as many other aspects of decision-making, see H. Simon, *Administrative Behavior: A Study of Decision-Making Processes in Administrative Organizations* (1947; 4th edn., New York: The Free Press, 1997) and H. Simon, 'Rationality as a Process and Product of Thought', *American Economic Review*, Vol. 68 (1978): 1–16.

On the coalitional model of decision-making, see J. March, 'The Business Firm as a Political Coalition', *Journal of Politics*, Vol. 24/4 (1962): 662–78.

Resource dependency theory was proposed by J. Pfeffer and J. Salancik, *The External Control of Organizations: A Resource Dependence Perspective* (Stanford, CA: Stanford University Press, 1978).

Read more about inequity in J. Acker, *Doing Comparable Worth: Gender, Class and Pay Equity* (Philadelphia: Temple University Press, 1991). For her ideas on gendered organizations, read her chapter in M. M. Ferree and P. Y. Martin, *Feminist Organizations: Harvest of the New Women's Movement* (Philadelphia, PA: Temple University Press, 1995), pp. 137–44.

Information about the Kabyle is taken from P. Bourdieu, 'The Kabyle House or the World Reversed', in P. Bourdieu, *Algeria 1960: The Disenchantment of the World, the Sense of Honor, the Kabyle House or the World Reversed* (Studies in Modern Capitalism, Cambridge, UK: Cambridge University Press, 1979).

For critique of Enlightenment reasoning, see J.-F. Lyotard, *The Postmodern Condition: A Report on Knowledge*, tr. G. Bennington and B. Massumi (Minneapolis, MN: University of Minnesota Press, 1979). For more on truth claims, see J.-F. Lyotard, *The Differend: Phrases in Dispute*, tr. G. Van den Abeele (Minneapolis, MN: University of Minnesota Press, 1983).

M. Foucault, *Discipline and Punish: The Birth of the Prison* (1975, in French as *Surveiller et punir: Naissance de la Prison*; tr. A. Sheridan, New York: Vintage, 1980) defines disciplinary power and illustrates it through analysis of prisons, institutions for the mentally insane, hospitals, and schools.

The Texas Board of Education story from R. Shorto, 'How Christian Were the Founders?', *New York Times Magazine*, (11 February 2010); full text can be found at http://www.nytimes.com/2010/02/14/magazine/14texbooks-t.html, accessed 11 November 2010.

## Chapter 5

Several different developmental models of organizational growth and
   change exist. The one presented here is taken from D. Katz and
   R. L. Kahn, *The Social Psychology of Organizations* (New York:
   Wiley, 1966). For another popular developmental model, see
   L. Greiner, 'Evolution and Revolution as Organizations Grow',
   *Harvard Business Review*, Vol. 50 (1972): 37–46.

The example of Orion's Belts is loosely based on experiences related
   to me many years ago by an old friend, one of the co-founders of
   the company. There are undoubtedly many inaccuracies in my
   recollection, and I did not attempt to verify the material with any
   of the participants; the material is presented solely for the purpose
   of illustrating Katz and Kahn's model of organizational
   development stages and not to document the case.

J. Dewey, *Art as Experience* (1934; New York: Perigee, Putnam's Sons,
   1980).

The original models of culture and identity dynamics can be found in
   M. J. Hatch, 'The Dynamics of Organizational Culture', *Academy of
   Management Review*, 18 (1993): 657–93, and M. J. Hatch and
   M. Schultz, 'The Dynamics of Organizational Identity', *Human
   Relations*, Vol. 55 (2002): 989–1018. The combined model will be
   found in M. J. Hatch, 'Material and Meaning in the Dynamics of
   Organizational Culture and Identity with Implications for the
   Leadership of Organizational Change', in N. Ashkanasy, C.
   Wilderom, and M. Peterson (eds.), *The Handbook of
   Organizational Culture and Climate*, 2nd edn. (London: Sage,
   2010): 341–58. The models shown in Figure 19 come from M. J.
   Hatch and M. Schultz, *Taking Brand Initiative: How Corporations
   Can Align Strategy, Culture and Identity through Corporate
   Branding* (San Francisco, CA: Wiley/Jossey-Bass, 2008).

The McDonald's example comes from personal communication with
   a former employee of the company. You can read much about the
   ongoing critical debate on websites such as http://www.
   sourcewatch.org/index.php?title=McDonald's, accessed 11
   November 2010.

For organizational network theory, see N. Nohria and R. Eccles, *Networks
   in Oranizations*, 2nd edn. (Boston, MA: Harvard Business School
   Press, 1992). For a classic, read Mark Granovetter, 'The Strength of
   Weak Ties', *American Journal of Sociology*, Vol. 78 (1973): 1360–80.

Action nets are opposed to actor network theory (ANT), a popular sociological view. On action nets, read B. Czarniawska's 'On Time, Space and Action Nets', *Organization*, Vol. 11/6 (2004): 773–91. On ANT, read B. LaTour, *Reassembling the Social: An Introduction to Actor Network Theory* (Oxford: Oxford University Press, 2005).

## Chapter 6

The example of IBM's Service Corp., as well as other ideas about CSR and corporate citizenship, come from Bradley Googins, Philip Mirvis, and Steve Rochlin, *Beyond Good Company: Next Generation Corporate Citizenship* (New York: Palgrave, 2007).

Base and superstructure concepts are from K. Marx, *A Contribution to the Critique of Political Economy* (1859; Moscow: Progress Publishers, 1977). 'All that is solid' quote can be found in K. Marx and F. Engels, 'Bourgeoisie and Proletarians', *The Communist Manifesto* (1848; full text at http://www.apu.ac.jp/~jse/THE%20COMMUNIST%20MANIFESTO.htm, accessed 11 November 2010).

An accessible entrée to the new physics of superstring theory is provided by M. Kaku, *Hyperspace: A Scientific Odyssey through the Tenth Dimension* (Oxford: Oxford University Press, 1994). On links between the new physics and spirituality, read A. Zajonc (ed.), *The New Physics and Cosmology: Dialogues with the Dalai Lama* (Oxford: Oxford University Press, 2004).

Nissan example taken from M. J. Hatch and M. Schultz, *Taking Brand Initiative: How Corporations Can Align Strategy, Culture and Identity through Corporate Branding* (San Francisco, CA: Wiley/Jossey-Bass, 2008).

For more about jazz as a metaphor for organizing, see M. J. Hatch, 'Exploring the Empty Spaces of Organizing: How Improvisational Jazz Helps Redescribe Organizational Structure', *Organization Studies*, Vol. 20 (1999): 75–100.

## Appendix

É. Durkheim, *Suicide: A Study in Sociology* (New York: The Free Press, 1951).

R. Weber, 'The Rhetoric of Positivism versus Interpretivism: A Personal View', *MIS Quarterly*, 28/1 (2004): iii–xii. Text can

be found at: http://www.misq.org/archivist/vol/no28/
issue1/EdCommentsV28N1.pdf accessed 11 November 2010.

Quotation from M. Heidegger, *On the Way to Language* (New York: Harper & Row, 1971), p. 101.

The linguistic turn had many antecedents and sources, only three of which I mention here. The primary source for the notion of discourse is M. Foucault, *The Order of Things* (London: Pantheon, 1970). Speech act theory did much to inspire the idea that language can enact reality (e.g. 'I thee wed'); on this, see J. L. Austin, *'How To Do Things with Words'*, *The William James Lectures delivered at Harvard University in 1955*, ed. J. O. Urmson (Oxford: Clarendon Press, 1962). The instability of meaning was a view propounded by J. Derrida, *Writing and Difference*, tr. Alan Bass (Chicag, IL: University of Chicago Press, 1978).

J. Habermas, *The Theory of Communicative Action*, Vol. 1: *Reason and the Rationalization of Society*, tr. T. McCarthy (Boston, MA: Beacon Press, 1984).

H. Tsoukas and R. Chia, 'Organizational Becoming: Rethinking Organizational Change', *Organization Science*, Vol. 13/5 (2002): 567–82.

W. B. Yeats, 'Among School Children', found at: http://athome. harvard.edu/programs/vendler/vendler_segment6_set.html, accessed 11 November 2010.

# Further reading

## Organizations, general

B. Czarniawska, *A Theory of Organizing* (Cheltenham, UK: Edward Elgar, 2008)

M. J. Hatch (with A. Cunliffe), *Organization Theory: Modern, Symbolic and Postmodern Perspectives*, 2nd edn. (Oxford: Oxford University Press, 2006)

## Systems theory

L. Von Bertalanffy, *General System Theory: Foundations, Development, Applications* (1968; New York: George Braziller, 1976)

## Capitalism and globalization

N. Ferguson, *Empire: The Rise and Demise of the British World Order and the Lessons for Global Power* (London: Basic Books, 2002)

N. Ferguson, *Colossus: The Price of America's Empire* (New York: Penguin, 2004)

## Technology and innovation

S. Burns and G. M. Stalker, *The Management of Innovation* (London: Tavistock, 1961)

C. Perrow, *Normal Accidents: Living with High Risk Technologies* (1984, Basic Books; Princeton, NJ: Princeton University Press, 1999)

## Organizational environments and contingency theory

H. Aldrich, *Organizations and Environments* (Palo Alto, CA: Stanford University Press, 2007)

L. Donaldson, *The Contingency Theory of Organizations* (Thousand Oaks, CA: Sage, 2001)

## Organizational institutionalism and social movements

R. Greenwood, C. Oliver, K. Sahlin, and R. Suddaby, *Sage Handbook of Organizational Institutionalism* (London: Sage, 2008)

W. R. Scott, *Institutions and Organizations* (Thousand Oaks, CA: Sage, 2001)

G. F. Davis, D. McAdam, W. R. Scott, and M. N. Zald (eds.), *Social Movements and Organization Theory* (New York: Cambridge University Press, 2005)

## Organizational culture

N. Ashkanasy, C. Wilderom, and M. Peterson (eds.), *The Handbook of Organizational Culture and Climate*, 2nd edn. (Thousand Oaks, CA: Sage, 2010)

J. Martin, *Cultures in Organizations: Three Perspectives* (New York: Oxford University Press, 1992)

E. Schein, *Organizational Culture and Leadership*, 3rd edn. (San Francisco, CA: Jossey-Bass, 1992)

## Power

S. Clegg, D. Courpasson, and N. Phillips, *Power and Organizations* (London: Sage, 2006)

J. Pfeffer, *Managing with Power: Politics and Influence in Organizations* (Cambridge, MA: Harvard Business School Press, 1992)

## Feminist theory

C. Gilligan, *In a Different Voice: Psychological Theory and Women's Development* (Cambridge, MA: Harvard University Press, 1993)

## Organizational identity

Many classic articles on organizational identity, including the excerpt from G. H. Mead's work on social identity, can be found in

M. J. Hatch and M. Schultz (eds.), *Organizational Identity: A Reader* (Oxford: Oxford University Press, 2004)

B. Czarniawska, *Narrating the Organization: Dramas of Institutional Identity* (Chicago, IL: University of Chicago Press, 1997)

## Complexity theory and social networks

S. Kauffman, *At Home in the Universe: The Search for Laws of Complexity* (Harmondsworth: Penguin, 1995)

D. J. Watts, *Six Degrees: The Science of a Connected Age* (New York: W. W. Norton, 2003)

R. A. Axelrod and M. D. Cohen, *Harnessing Complexity: Organizational Implications of a Scientific Frontier* (New York: Free Press, 2000)

## Process theories of organizing

The Perspectives on Process Organization Studies series edited by H. Tsoukas and A. Langley provides annual volumes devoted to process research in organizations. The first is T. Hernes and S. Maitlis, *Process, Sensemaking and Organizing* (Oxford: Oxford University Press, 2010)

# Index

# Expand your collection of
# VERY SHORT INTRODUCTIONS